THE POETICS (annotated)

By Aristotle

A TRANSLATION BY S. H. Butcher

[Transcriber's Annotations and Conventions: the translator left intact some Greek words to illustrate a specific point of the original discourse. In this transcription, in order to retain the accuracy of this text, those words are rendered by spelling out each Greek letter individually, such as {alpha beta gamma delta ...}. The reader can distinguish these words by the enclosing braces {}. Where multiple words occur together, they are separated by the "/" symbol for clarity. Readers who do not speak or read the Greek language will usually neither gain nor lose understanding by skipping over these passages. Those who understand Greek, however, may gain a deeper insight to the original meaning and distinctions expressed by Aristotle.]

Analysis of Contents

disastrous Incident defined and explained.

Tragedy.

I

I propose to treat of Poetry in itself and of its various kinds, noting the essential quality of each; to inquire into the structure of the plot as requisite to a good poem; into the number and nature of the parts of which a poem is composed; and similarly into whatever else falls within the same inquiry. Following, then, the order of nature, let us begin with the principles which come first.

Epic poetry and Tragedy, Comedy also and Dithyrambic: poetry, and the music of the flute and of the lyre in most of their forms, are all in their general conception modes of imitation. They differ, however, from one: another in three respects,--the medium, the objects, the manner or mode of imitation, being in each case distinct.

For as there are persons who, by conscious art or mere habit, imitate and represent various objects through the medium of colour and form, or again by the voice; so in the arts above mentioned, taken as a whole, the imitation is produced by rhythm, language, or 'harmony,' either singly or combined.

Thus in the music of the flute and of the lyre, 'harmony' and rhythm alone are employed; also in other arts, such as that of the shepherd's pipe, which are essentially similar to these. In dancing, rhythm alone is used without 'harmony'; for even dancing imitates character, emotion, and action, by rhythmical movement.

There is another art which imitates by means of language alone, and that either in prose or verse--which, verse, again, may either combine different metres or consist of but one kind--but this has hitherto been without a name. For there is no common term we could apply to the mimes of Sophron and Xenarchus and the Socratic dialogues on the one hand; and, on the other, to poetic imitations in iambic, elegiac, or any similar metre. People do, indeed, add the word 'maker' or 'poet' to the name of the metre, and speak of elegiac poets, or epic (that is, hexameter) poets, as if it were not the imitation that makes the poet, but the verse that entitles them all indiscriminately to the name. Even when a treatise on medicine or natural science is brought out in verse, the name of poet is by custom given to the author; and yet Homer and Empedocles have nothing in common but the metre, so that it would be right to call the one poet, the other physicist rather than poet. On the same principle, even if a writer in his poetic imitation were to combine all metres, as Chaeremon did in his Centaur, which is a medley composed of metres of all kinds, we should bring him too under the general term poet. So much then for these distinctions.

There are, again, some arts which employ all the means above mentioned, namely, rhythm, tune, and metre. Such are Dithyrambic and Nomic poetry, and also Tragedy and Comedy; but between them the difference is, that in the first two cases these means are all employed in combination, in the latter, now one means is employed, now another.

Such, then, are the differences of the arts with respect to the medium of imitation.

II

Since the objects of imitation are men in action, and these men must be either of a higher or a lower type (for moral character mainly answers to these divisions, goodness and badness being the distinguishing marks of moral differences), it follows that we must represent men either as better than in real life, or as worse, or as they are. It is the same in painting. Polygnotus depicted men as nobler than they are, Pauson as less noble, Dionysius drew them true to life.

Now it is evident that each of the modes of imitation above mentioned will exhibit these differences, and become a distinct kind in imitating objects that are thus distinct. Such diversities may be found even in dancing,: flute-playing, and lyre-playing. So again in language, whether prose or verse unaccompanied by music. Homer, for example, makes men better than they are; Cleophon as they are; Hegemon the Thasian, the inventor of parodies, and Nicochares, the author of the Deiliad, worse than they are. The same thing holds good of Dithyrambs and Nomes; here too one may portray different types, as Timotheus and Philoxenus differed in representing their Cyclopes. The same distinction marks off Tragedy from Comedy; for Comedy aims at representing men as worse, Tragedy as better than in actual life.

III

There is still a third difference--the manner in which each of these objects may be imitated. For the medium being the same, and the objects the same, the poet may imitate by narration--in which case he can either take another personality as Homer does, or speak in his own person, unchanged--or he may present all his characters as living and moving before us.

These, then, as we said at the beginning, are the three differences which distinguish artistic imitation,--the medium, the objects, and the manner. So that from one point of view, Sophocles is an imitator of the same kind as Homer--for both imitate higher types of character; from another point of view, of the same kind as Aristophanes--for both imitate persons acting and doing. Hence, some say, the name of 'drama' is given to such poems, as representing action. For the same reason the Dorians claim the invention both of Tragedy and Comedy. The claim to Comedy is put forward by the Megarians,--not only by those of Greece proper, who allege that it originated under their democracy, but also by the Megarians of Sicily, for the poet Epicharmus, who is much earlier than Chionides and Magnes, belonged to that country. Tragedy too is claimed by certain Dorians of the Peloponnese. In each case they appeal to the evidence of language. The outlying villages, they say, are by them called {kappa omega mu alpha iota}, by the Athenians {delta eta mu iota}: and they assume that Comedians were so named not from {kappa omega mu 'alpha zeta epsilon iota nu}, 'to revel,' but because they wandered from village to village (kappa alpha tau alpha / kappa omega mu alpha sigma), being excluded contemptuously from the city. They add also that the Dorian word for 'doing' is {delta rho alpha nu}, and the Athenian, {pi rho alpha tau tau epsilon iota nu}.

This may suffice as to the number and nature of the various modes of imitation.

IV

Poetry in general seems to have sprung from two causes, each of them lying deep in our nature. First, the instinct of imitation is implanted in man from childhood, one difference between him and other animals being that he is the most imitative of living creatures, and through imitation learns his earliest lessons; and no less universal is the pleasure felt in things imitated. We have evidence of this in the facts of experience. Objects which in themselves we view with pain, we delight to contemplate when reproduced with minute fidelity: such as the forms of the most ignoble animals and of dead bodies. The cause of this again is, that to learn gives the liveliest pleasure, not only to philosophers but to men in general; whose capacity, however, of learning is more limited. Thus the reason why men enjoy seeing a likeness is, that in contemplating it they find themselves learning or inferring, and saying perhaps, 'Ah, that is he.' For if you happen not to have seen the original, the pleasure will be due not to the imitation as such, but to the execution, the colouring, or some such other cause.

Imitation, then, is one instinct of our nature. Next, there is the instinct for 'harmony' and rhythm, metres being manifestly sections of rhythm. Persons, therefore, starting with this natural gift developed by degrees their special aptitudes, till their rude improvisations gave birth to Poetry.

Poetry now diverged in two directions, according to the individual character of the writers. The graver spirits imitated noble actions, and the actions of good men. The more trivial sort imitated the actions of meaner persons, at first composing satires, as the former did hymns to the gods and the praises of famous men. A poem of the satirical kind cannot indeed be put down to any author earlier than Homer; though many such writers probably there were. But from Homer onward, instances can be cited,--his own Margites, for example, and other similar compositions. The appropriate metre was also here introduced; hence the measure is still called the iambic or lampooning measure, being that in which people lampooned one another. Thus the older poets were distinguished as writers of heroic or of lampooning verse.

As, in the serious style, Homer is pre-eminent among poets, for he alone combined dramatic form with excellence of imitation, so he too first laid down the main lines of Comedy, by dramatising the ludicrous instead of writing personal satire. His Margites bears the same relation to Comedy that the Iliad and Odyssey do to Tragedy. But when Tragedy and Comedy came to light, the two classes of poets still followed their natural bent: the lampooners became writers of Comedy, and the Epic poets were succeeded by Tragedians, since the drama was a larger and higher form of art.

Whether Tragedy has as yet perfected its proper types or not; and whether it is to be judged in itself, or in relation also to the audience,--this raises another question. Be that as it may, Tragedy--as also Comedy --- was at first mere improvisation. The one originated with the authors of the Dithyramb, the other with those of the phallic songs, which are still in use in many of our cities. Tragedy advanced by slow degrees; each new element that showed itself was in turn developed. Having passed through many changes, it found its natural form, and there it stopped.

Aeschylus first introduced a second actor; he diminished the importance of the Chorus, and assigned the leading part to the dialogue. Sophocles raised the number of actors to three, and added scene-painting. Moreover, it was not till late that the short plot was discarded for one of greater compass, and the grotesque diction of the earlier satyric form for the stately manner of Tragedy. The iambic measure then replaced the trochaic tetrameter, which was originally employed when the poetry was of the Satyric order, and had greater affinities with dancing. Once dialogue had come in, Nature herself discovered the appropriate measure. For the iambic is, of all measures, the most colloquial: we see it in the fact that conversational speech runs into iambic lines more frequently than into any other kind of verse; rarely into hexameters, and only when we drop the colloquial intonation. The additions to the number of 'episodes' or acts, and the other accessories of which tradition; tells, must be taken as already described; for to discuss them in detail would, doubtless, be a large undertaking.

V

Comedy is, as we have said, an imitation of characters of a lower type, not, however, in the full sense of the word bad, the Ludicrous being merely a subdivision of the ugly. It consists in some defect or ugliness which is not painful or destructive. To take an obvious example, the comic mask is ugly and distorted, but does not imply pain.

The successive changes through which Tragedy passed, and the authors of these changes, are well known, whereas Comedy has had no history, because it was not at first treated seriously. It was late before the Archon granted a comic chorus to a poet; the performers were till then voluntary. Comedy had already taken definite shape when comic poets, distinctively so called, are heard of. Who furnished it with masks, or prologues, or increased the number of actors,--these and other similar details remain unknown. As for the plot, it came originally from Sicily; but of Athenian writers Crates was the first who, abandoning the 'iambic' or lampooning form, generalised his themes and plots.

Epic poetry agrees with Tragedy in so far as it is an imitation in verse of characters of a higher type. They differ, in that Epic poetry admits but one kind of metre, and is narrative in form. They differ, again, in their length: for Tragedy endeavours, as far as possible, to confine itself to a single revolution of the sun, or but slightly to exceed this limit; whereas the Epic action has no limits of time. This, then, is a second point of difference; though at first the same freedom was admitted in Tragedy as in Epic poetry.

Of their constituent parts some are common to both, some peculiar to Tragedy, whoever, therefore, knows what is good or bad Tragedy, knows also about Epic poetry. All the elements of an Epic poem are found in Tragedy, but the elements of a Tragedy are not all found in the Epic poem.

VI

Of the poetry which imitates in hexameter verse, and of Comedy, we will speak hereafter. Let us now discuss Tragedy, resuming its formal definition, as resulting from what has been already said.

Tragedy, then, is an imitation of an action that is serious, complete, and of a certain magnitude; in language embellished with each kind of artistic ornament, the several kinds being found in separate parts of the play; in the form of action, not of narrative; through pity and fear effecting the proper purgation of these emotions. By 'language embellished,' I mean language into which rhythm, 'harmony,' and song enter. By 'the several kinds in separate parts,' I mean, that some parts are rendered through the medium of verse alone, others again with the aid of song.

Now as tragic imitation implies persons acting, it necessarily follows, in the first place, that Spectacular equipment will be a part of Tragedy. Next, Song and Diction, for these are the medium of imitation. By 'Diction' I mean the mere metrical arrangement of the words: as for 'Song,' it is a term whose sense every one understands.

Again, Tragedy is the imitation of an action; and an action implies personal agents, who necessarily possess certain distinctive qualities both of character and thought; for it is by these that we qualify actions themselves, and these--thought and character--are the two natural causes from which actions spring, and on actions again all success or failure depends. Hence, the Plot is the imitation of the action: for by plot I here mean the arrangement of the incidents. By Character I mean that in virtue of which we ascribe certain qualities to the agents. Thought is required wherever a statement is proved, or, it may be, a general truth enunciated. Every Tragedy, therefore, must have six parts, which parts determine its quality--namely, Plot, Character, Diction, Thought, Spectacle, Song. Two of the parts constitute the medium of imitation, one the manner, and three the objects of imitation. And these complete the list. These elements have been employed, we may say, by the poets to a man; in fact, every play contains Spectacular elements as well as Character, Plot, Diction, Song, and Thought.

But most important of all is the structure of the incidents. For Tragedy is an imitation, not of men, but of an action and of life, and life consists in action, and its end is a mode of action, not a quality. Now character determines men's qualities, but it is by their actions that they are happy or the reverse. Dramatic action, therefore, is not with a view to the representation of character: character comes in as subsidiary to the actions. Hence the incidents and the plot are the end of a tragedy; and the end is the chief thing of all. Again, without action there cannot be a tragedy; there may be without character. The tragedies of most of our modern poets fail in the rendering of character; and of poets in general this is often true. It is the same in painting; and here lies the difference between Zeuxis and Polygnotus. Polygnotus delineates character well: the style of Zeuxis is devoid of ethical quality. Again, if you string together a set of speeches expressive of character, and well finished in point of diction and thought, you will not produce the essential tragic effect nearly so well as with a play which, however deficient in these respects, yet has a plot and artistically constructed incidents. Besides which, the most powerful elements of emotional: interest in Tragedy Peripeteia or Reversal of the Situation, and Recognition scenes--are parts of the plot. A further proof is, that novices in the art attain to finish: of diction and precision of portraiture before they can construct the plot. It is the same with almost all the early poets.

The Plot, then, is the first principle, and, as it were, the soul of a tragedy: Character holds the second place. A similar fact is seen in painting. The most beautiful colours, laid on confusedly, will not give as much pleasure as the chalk outline of a portrait. Thus Tragedy is the imitation of an action, and of the agents mainly with a view to the action.

Third in order is Thought,--that is, the faculty of saying what is possible and pertinent in given circumstances. In the case of oratory, this is the function of the Political art and of the art of rhetoric: and so indeed the older poets make their characters speak the language of civic life; the poets of our time, the language of the rhetoricians. Character is that which reveals moral purpose, showing what kind of things a man chooses or avoids. Speeches, therefore, which do not make this manifest, or in which the speaker does not choose or avoid anything whatever, are not expressive of character. Thought, on the other hand, is found where something is proved to be. or not to be, or a general maxim is enunciated.

Fourth among the elements enumerated comes Diction; by which I mean, as has been already said, the expression of the meaning in words; and its essence is the same both in verse and prose.

Of the remaining elements Song holds the chief place among the embellishments.

The Spectacle has, indeed, an emotional attraction of its own, but, of all the parts, it is the least artistic, and connected least with the art of poetry. For the power of Tragedy, we may be sure, is felt even apart from representation and actors. Besides, the production of spectacular effects depends more on the art of the stage machinist than on that of the poet.

VII

These principles being established, let us now discuss the proper structure of the Plot, since this is the first and most important thing in Tragedy.

Now, according to our definition, Tragedy is an imitation of an action that is complete, and whole, and of a certain magnitude; for there may be a whole that is wanting in magnitude. A whole is that which has a beginning, a middle, and an end. A beginning is that which does not itself follow anything by causal necessity, but after which something naturally is or comes to be. An end, on the contrary, is that which itself naturally follows some other thing, either by necessity, or as a rule, but has nothing following it. A middle is that which follows something as some other thing follows it. A well constructed plot, therefore, must neither begin nor end at haphazard, but conform to these principles.

Again, a beautiful object, whether it be a living organism or any whole composed of parts, must not only have an orderly arrangement of parts, but must also be of a certain magnitude; for beauty depends on magnitude and order. Hence a very small animal organism cannot be beautiful; for the view of it is confused, the object being seen in an almost imperceptible moment of time. Nor, again, can one of vast size be beautiful; for as the eye cannot take it all in at once, the unity and sense of the whole is lost for the spectator; as for instance if there were one a thousand miles long. As, therefore, in the case of animate bodies and organisms a certain magnitude is necessary, and a magnitude which may be easily embraced in one view; so in the plot, a certain length is necessary, and a length which can be easily embraced by the memory. The limit of length in relation to dramatic competition and sensuous presentment, is no part of artistic theory. For had it been the rule for a hundred tragedies to compete together, the performance would have been regulated by the water-clock,--as indeed we are told was formerly done. But the limit as fixed by the nature of the drama itself is this: the greater the length, the more beautiful will the piece be by reason of its size, provided that the whole be perspicuous. And to define the matter roughly, we may say that the proper magnitude is comprised within such limits, that the sequence of events, according to the law of probability or necessity, will admit of a change from bad fortune to good, or from good fortune to bad.

VIII

Unity of plot does not, as some persons think, consist in the Unity of the hero. For infinitely various are the incidents in one man's life which cannot be reduced to unity; and so, too, there are many actions of one man out of which we cannot make one action. Hence, the error, as it appears, of all poets who have composed a Heracleid, a Theseid, or other poems of the kind. They imagine that as Heracles was one man, the story of Heracles must also be a unity. But Homer, as in all else he is of surpassing merit, here too--whether from art or natural genius--seems to have happily discerned the truth. In composing the Odyssey he did not include all the adventures of Odysseus-- such as his wound on Parnassus, or his feigned madness at the mustering of the host--incidents between which there was no necessary or probable connection: but he made the Odyssey, and likewise the Iliad, to centre round an action that in our sense of the word is one. As therefore, in the other imitative arts, the imitation is one when the object imitated is one, so the plot, being an imitation of an action, must imitate one action and that a whole, the structural union of the parts being such that, if any one of them is displaced or removed, the whole will be disjointed and disturbed. For a thing whose presence or absence makes no visible difference, is not an organic part of the whole.

IX

It is, moreover, evident from what has been said, that it is not the function of the poet to relate what has happened, but what may happen,-- what is possible according to the law of probability or necessity. The poet and the historian differ not by writing in verse or in prose. The work of Herodotus might be put into verse, and it would still be a species of history, with metre no less than without it. The true difference is that one relates what has happened, the other what may happen. Poetry, therefore, is a more philosophical and a higher thing than history: for poetry tends to express the universal, history the particular. By the universal, I mean how a person of a certain type will on occasion speak or act, according to the law of probability or necessity; and it is this universality at which poetry aims in the names she attaches to the personages. The particular is--for example--what Alcibiades did or suffered. In Comedy this is already apparent: for here the poet first constructs the plot on the lines of probability, and then inserts characteristic names;--unlike the lampooners who write about particular individuals. But tragedians still keep to real names, the reason being that what is possible is credible: what has not happened we do not at once feel sure to be possible: but what has happened is manifestly possible: otherwise it would not have happened. Still there are even some tragedies in which there are only one or two well known names, the rest being fictitious. In others, none are well known, as in Agathon's Antheus, where incidents and names alike are fictitious, and yet they give none the less pleasure. We must not, therefore, at all costs keep to the received legends, which are the usual subjects of Tragedy. Indeed, it would be absurd to attempt it; for even subjects that are known are known only to a few, and yet give pleasure to all. It clearly follows that the poet or 'maker' should be the maker of plots rather than of verses; since he is a poet because he imitates, and what he imitates are actions. And even if he chances to take an historical subject, he is none the less a poet; for there is no reason why some events that have actually happened should not conform to the law of the probable and possible, and in virtue of that quality in them he is their poet or maker.

Of all plots and actions the epeisodic are the worst. I call a plot 'epeisodic' in which the episodes or acts succeed one another without probable or necessary sequence. Bad poets compose such pieces by their own fault, good poets, to please the players; for, as they write show pieces for competition, they stretch the plot beyond its capacity, and are often forced to break the natural continuity.

But again, Tragedy is an imitation not only of a complete action, but of events inspiring fear or pity. Such an effect is best produced when the events come on us by sunrise; and the effect is heightened when, at the same time, they follow as cause and effect. The tragic wonder will thee be greater than if they happened of themselves or by accident; for even coincidences are most striking when they have an air of design. We may instance the statue of Mitys at Argos, which fell upon his murderer while he was a spectator at a festival, and killed him. Such events seem not to be due to mere chance. Plots, therefore, constructed on these principles are necessarily the best.

X

Plots are either Simple or Complex, for the actions in real life, of which the plots are an imitation, obviously show a similar distinction. An action which is one and continuous in the sense above defined, I call Simple, when the change of fortune takes place without Reversal of the Situation and without Recognition.

A Complex action is one in which the change is accompanied by such Reversal, or by Recognition, or by both. These last should arise from the internal structure of the plot, so that what follows should be the necessary or probable result of the preceding action. It makes all the difference whether any given event is a case of propter hoc or post hoc.

XI

Reversal of the Situation is a change by which the action veers round to its opposite, subject always to our rule of probability or necessity. Thus in the Oedipus, the messenger comes to cheer Oedipus and free him from his alarms about his mother, but by revealing who he is, he produces the opposite effect. Again in the Lynceus, Lynceus is being led away to his death, and Danaus goes with him, meaning, to slay him; but the outcome of the preceding incidents is that Danaus is killed and Lynceus saved. Recognition, as the name indicates, is a change from ignorance to knowledge, producing love or hate between the persons destined by the poet for good or bad fortune. The best form of recognition is coincident with a Reversal of the Situation, as in the Oedipus. There are indeed other forms. Even inanimate things of the most trivial kind may in a sense be objects of recognition. Again, we may recognise or discover whether a person has done a thing or not. But the recognition which is most intimately connected with the plot and action is, as we have said, the recognition of persons. This recognition, combined, with Reversal, will produce either pity or fear; and actions producing these effects are those which, by our definition, Tragedy represents. Moreover, it is upon such situations that the issues of good or bad fortune will depend. Recognition, then, being between persons, it may happen that one person only is recognised by the other-when the latter is already known--or it may be necessary that the recognition should be on both sides. Thus Iphigenia is revealed to Orestes by the sending of the letter; but another act of recognition is required to make Orestes known to Iphigenia.

Two parts, then, of the Plot--Reversal of the Situation and Recognition-- turn upon surprises. A third part is the Scene of Suffering. The Scene of Suffering is a destructive or painful action, such as death on the stage, bodily agony, wounds and the like.

XII

[The parts of Tragedy which must be treated as elements of the whole have been already mentioned. We now come to the quantitative parts, and the separate parts into which Tragedy is divided, namely, Prologue, Episode, Exode, Choric song; this last being divided into Parode and Stasimon. These are common to all plays: peculiar to some are the songs of actors from the stage and the Commoi.

The Prologue is that entire part of a tragedy which precedes the Parode of the Chorus. The Episode is that entire part of a tragedy which is between complete choric songs. The Exode is that entire part of a tragedy which has no choric song after it. Of the Choric part the Parode is the first undivided utterance of the Chorus: the Stasimon is a Choric ode without anapaests or trochaic tetrameters: the Commos is a joint lamentation of Chorus and actors. The parts of Tragedy which must be treated as elements of the whole have been already mentioned. The quantitative parts the separate parts into which it is divided--are here enumerated.]

XIII

As the sequel to what has already been said, we must proceed to consider what the poet should aim at, and what he should avoid, in constructing his plots; and by what means the specific effect of Tragedy will be produced.

A perfect tragedy should, as we have seen, be arranged not on the simple but on the complex plan. It should, moreover, imitate actions which excite pity and fear, this being the distinctive mark of tragic imitation. It follows plainly, in the first place, that the change, of fortune presented must not be the spectacle of a virtuous man brought from prosperity to adversity: for this moves neither pity nor fear; it merely shocks us. Nor, again, that of a bad man passing from adversity to prosperity: for nothing can be more alien to the spirit of Tragedy; it possesses no single tragic quality; it neither satisfies the moral sense nor calls forth pity or fear. Nor, again, should the downfall of the utter villain be exhibited. A plot of this kind would, doubtless, satisfy the moral sense, but it would inspire neither pity nor fear; for pity is aroused by unmerited misfortune, fear by the misfortune of a man like ourselves. Such an event, therefore, will be neither pitiful nor terrible. There remains, then, the character between these two extremes,- -that of a man who is not eminently good and just,-yet whose misfortune is brought about not by vice or depravity, but by some error or frailty. He must be one who is highly renowned and prosperous,--a personage like Oedipus, Thyestes, or other illustrious men of such families.

A well constructed plot should, therefore, be single in its issue, rather than double as some maintain. The change of fortune should be not from bad to good, but, reversely, from good to bad. It should come about as the result not of vice, but of some great error or frailty, in a character either such as we have described, or better rather than worse. The practice of the stage bears out our view. At first the poets recounted any legend that came in their way. Now, the best tragedies are founded on the story of a few houses, on the fortunes of Alcmaeon, Oedipus, Orestes, Meleager, Thyestes, Telephus, and those others who have done or suffered something terrible. A tragedy, then, to be perfect according to the rules of art should be of this construction. Hence they are in error who censure Euripides just because he follows this principle in his plays, many of which end unhappily. It is, as we have said, the right ending. The best proof is that on the stage and in dramatic competition, such plays, if well worked out, are the most tragic in effect; and Euripides, faulty though he may be in the general management of his subject, yet is felt to be the most tragic of the poets.

In the second rank comes the kind of tragedy which some place first. Like the Odyssey, it has a double thread of plot, and also an opposite catastrophe for the good and for the bad. It is accounted the best because of the weakness of the spectators; for the poet is guided in what he writes by the wishes of his audience. The pleasure, however, thence derived is not the true tragic pleasure. It is proper rather to Comedy, where those who, in the piece, are the deadliest enemies---like Orestes and Aegisthus--quit the stage as friends at the close, and no one slays or is slain.

XIV

Fear and pity may be aroused by spectacular means; but they may also result from the inner structure of the piece, which is the better way, and indicates a superior poet. For the plot ought to be so constructed that, even without the aid of the eye, he who hears the tale told will thrill with horror and melt to pity at what takes place. This is the impression we should receive from hearing the story of the Oedipus. But to produce this effect by the mere spectacle is a less artistic method, and dependent on extraneous aids. Those who employ spectacular means to create a sense not of the terrible but only of the monstrous, are strangers to the purpose of Tragedy; for we must not demand of Tragedy any and every kind of pleasure, but only that which is proper to it. And since the pleasure which the poet should afford is that which comes from pity and fear through imitation, it is evident that this quality must be impressed upon the incidents.

Let us then determine what are the circumstances which strike us as terrible or pitiful.

Actions capable of this effect must happen between persons who are either friends or enemies or indifferent to one another. If an enemy kills an enemy, there is nothing to excite pity either in the act or the intention, --except so far as the suffering in itself is pitiful. So again with indifferent persons. But when the tragic incident occurs between those who are near or dear to one another--if, for example, a brother kills, or intends to kill, a brother, a son his father, a mother her son, a son his mother, or any other deed of the kind is done---these are the situations to be looked for by the poet. He may not indeed destroy the framework of the received legends--the fact, for instance, that Clytemnestra was slain by Orestes and Eriphyle by Alcmaeon but he ought to show invention of his own, and skilfully handle the traditional material. Let us explain more clearly what is meant by skilful handling.

The action may be done consciously and with knowledge of the persons, in the manner of the older poets. It is thus too that Euripides makes Medea slay her children. Or, again, the deed of horror may be done, but done in ignorance, and the tie of kinship or friendship be discovered afterwards. The Oedipus of Sophocles is an example. Here, indeed, the incident is outside the drama proper; but cases occur where it falls within the action of the play: one may cite the Alcmaeon of Astydamas, or Telegonus in the Wounded Odysseus. Again, there is a third case,--<to be about to act with knowledge of the persons and then not to act. The fourth case is> when some one is about to do an irreparable deed through ignorance, and makes the discovery before it is done. These are the only possible ways. For the deed must either be done or not done,--and that wittingly or unwittingly. But of all these ways, to be about to act knowing the persons, and then not to act, is the worst. It is shocking without being tragic, for no disaster follows. It is, therefore, never, or very rarely, found in poetry. One instance, however, is in the Antigone, where Haemon threatens to kill Creon. The next and better way is that the deed should be perpetrated. Still better, that it should be perpetrated in ignorance, and the discovery made afterwards. There is then nothing to shock us, while the discovery produces a startling effect. The last case is the best, as when in the Cresphontes Merope is about to slay her son, but, recognising who he is, spares his life. So in the Iphigenia, the sister recognises the brother just in time. Again in the Helle, the son recognises the mother when on the point of giving her up. This, then, is why a few families only, as has been already observed, furnish the subjects of tragedy. It was not art, but happy chance, that led the poets in search of subjects to impress the tragic quality upon their plots. They are compelled, therefore, to have recourse to those houses whose history contains moving incidents like these.

Enough has now been said concerning the structure of the incidents, and the right kind of plot.

XV

In respect of Character there are four things to be aimed at. First, and most important, it must be good. Now any speech or action that manifests moral purpose of any kind will be expressive of character: the character will be good if the purpose is good. This rule is relative to each class. Even a woman may be good, and also a slave; though the woman may be said to be an inferior being, and the slave quite worthless. The second thing to aim at is propriety. There is a type of manly valour; but valour in a woman, or unscrupulous cleverness, is inappropriate. Thirdly, character must be true to life: for this is a distinct thing from goodness and propriety, as here described. The fourth point is consistency: for though the subject of the imitation, who suggested the type, be inconsistent, still he must be consistently inconsistent. As an example of motiveless degradation of character, we have Menelaus in the Orestes: of character indecorous and inappropriate, the lament of Odysseus in the Scylla, and the speech of Melanippe: of inconsistency, the Iphigenia at Aulis,--for Iphigenia the suppliant in no way resembles her later self.

As in the structure of the plot, so too in the portraiture of character, the poet should always aim either at the necessary or the probable. Thus a person of a given character should speak or act in a given way, by the rule either of necessity or of probability; just as this event should follow that by necessary or probable sequence. It is therefore evident that the unravelling of the plot, no less than the complication, must arise out of the plot itself, it must not be brought about by the 'Deus ex Machina'--as in the Medea, or in the Return of the Greeks in the Iliad. The 'Deus ex Machina' should be employed only for events external to the drama,--for antecedent or subsequent events, which lie beyond the range of human knowledge, and which require to be reported or foretold; for to the gods we ascribe the power of seeing all things. Within the action there must be nothing irrational. If the irrational cannot be excluded, it should be outside the scope of the tragedy. Such is the irrational element in the Oedipus of Sophocles.

Again, since Tragedy is an imitation of persons who are above the common level, the example of good portrait-painters should be followed. They, while reproducing the distinctive form of the original, make a likeness which is true to life and yet more beautiful. So too the poet, in representing men who are irascible or indolent, or have other defects of character, should preserve the type and yet ennoble it. In this way Achilles is portrayed by Agathon and Homer.

These then are rules the poet should observe. Nor should he neglect those appeals to the senses, which, though not among the essentials, are the concomitants of poetry; for here too there is much room for error. But of this enough has been said in our published treatises.

XVI

What Recognition is has been already explained. We will now enumerate its kinds.

First, the least artistic form, which, from poverty of wit, is most commonly employed recognition by signs. Of these some are congenital,-- such as 'the spear which the earth-born race bear on their bodies,' or the stars introduced by Carcinus in his Thyestes. Others are acquired after birth; and of these some are bodily marks, as scars; some external tokens, as necklaces, or the little ark in the Tyro by which the discovery is effected. Even these admit of more or less skilful treatment. Thus in the recognition of Odysseus by his scar, the discovery is made in one way by the nurse, in another by the swineherds. The use of tokens for the express purpose of proof --and, indeed, any formal proof with or without tokens --is a less artistic mode of recognition. A better kind is that which comes about by a turn of incident, as in the Bath Scene in the Odyssey.

Next come the recognitions invented at will by the poet, and on that account wanting in art. For example, Orestes in the Iphigenia reveals the fact that he is Orestes. She, indeed, makes herself known by the letter; but he, by speaking himself, and saying what the poet, not what the plot requires. This, therefore, is nearly allied to the fault above mentioned:--for Orestes might as well have brought tokens with him. Another similar instance is the 'voice of the shuttle' in the Tereus of Sophocles.

The third kind depends on memory when the sight of some object awakens a feeling: as in the Cyprians of Dicaeogenes, where the hero breaks into tears on seeing the picture; or again in the 'Lay of Alcinous,' where Odysseus, hearing the minstrel play the lyre, recalls the past and weeps; and hence the recognition.

The fourth kind is by process of reasoning. Thus in the Choephori: 'Some one resembling me has come: no one resembles me but Orestes: therefore Orestes has come.' Such too is the discovery made by Iphigenia in the play of Polyidus the Sophist. It was a natural reflection for Orestes to make, 'So I too must die at the altar like my sister.' So, again, in the Tydeus of Theodectes, the father says, 'I came to find my son, and I lose my own life.' So too in the Phineidae: the women, on seeing the place, inferred their fate:--'Here we are doomed to die, for here we were cast forth.' Again, there is a composite kind of recognition involving false inference on the part of one of the characters, as in the Odysseus Disguised as a Messenger. A said <that no one else was able to bend the bow; . . . hence B (the disguised Odysseus) imagined that A would> recognise the bow which, in fact, he had not seen; and to bring about a recognition by this means that the expectation A would recognise the bow is false inference.

But, of all recognitions, the best is that which arises from the incidents themselves, where the startling discovery is made by natural means. Such is that in the Oedipus of Sophocles, and in the Iphigenia; for it was natural that Iphigenia should wish to dispatch a letter. These recognitions alone dispense with the artificial aid of tokens or amulets. Next come the recognitions by process of reasoning.

XVII

In constructing the plot and working it out with the proper diction, the poet should place the scene, as far as possible, before his eyes. In this way, seeing everything with the utmost vividness, as if he were a spectator of the action, he will discover what is in keeping with it, and be most unlikely to overlook inconsistencies. The need of such a rule is shown by the fault found in Carcinus. Amphiaraus was on his way from the temple. This fact escaped the observation of one who did not see the situation. On the stage, however, the piece failed, the audience being offended at the oversight.

Again, the poet should work out his play, to the best of his power, with appropriate gestures; for those who feel emotion are most convincing through natural sympathy with the characters they represent; and one who is agitated storms, one who is angry rages, with the most life-like reality. Hence poetry implies either a happy gift of nature or a strain of madness. In the one case a man can take the mould of any character; in the other, he is lifted out of his proper self.

As for the story, whether the poet takes it ready made or constructs it for himself, he should first sketch its general outline, and then fill in the episodes and amplify in detail. The general plan may be illustrated by the Iphigenia. A young girl is sacrificed; she disappears mysteriously from the eyes of those who sacrificed her; She is transported to another country, where the custom is to offer up all strangers to the goddess. To this ministry she is appointed. Some time later her own brother chances to arrive. The fact that the oracle for some reason ordered him to go there, is outside the general plan of the play. The purpose, again, of his coming is outside the action proper. However, he comes, he is seized, and, when on the point of being sacrificed, reveals who he is. The mode of recognition may be either that of Euripides or of Polyidus, in whose play he exclaims very naturally:--'So it was not my sister only, but I too, who was doomed to be sacrificed'; and by that remark he is saved.

After this, the names being once given, it remains to fill in the episodes. We must see that they are relevant to the action. In the case of Orestes, for example, there is the madness which led to his capture, and his deliverance by means of the purificatory rite. In the drama, the episodes are short, but it is these that give extension to Epic poetry. Thus the story of the Odyssey can be stated briefly. A certain man is absent from home for many years; he is jealously watched by Poseidon, and left desolate. Meanwhile his home is in a wretched plight---suitors are wasting his substance and plotting against his son. At length, tempest- tost, he himself arrives; he makes certain persons acquainted with him; he attacks the suitors with his own hand, and is himself preserved while he destroys them. This is the essence of the plot; the rest is episode.

XVIII

Every tragedy falls into two parts,--Complication and Unravelling or Denouement. Incidents extraneous to the action are frequently combined with a portion of the action proper, to form the Complication; the rest is the Unravelling. By the Complication I mean all that extends from the beginning of the action to the part which marks the turning-point to good or bad fortune. The Unravelling is that which extends from the beginning of the change to the end. Thus, in the Lynceus of Theodectes, the Complication consists of the incidents presupposed in the drama, the seizure of the child, and then again * * <The Unravelling> extends from the accusation of murder to the end.

There are four kinds of Tragedy, the Complex, depending entirely on Reversal of the Situation and Recognition; the Pathetic (where the motive is passion),--such as the tragedies on Ajax and Ixion; the Ethical (where the motives are ethical),--such as the Phthiotides and the Peleus. The fourth kind is the Simple <We here exclude the purely spectacular element>, exemplified by the Phorcides, the Prometheus, and scenes laid in Hades. The poet should endeavour, if possible, to combine all poetic elements; or failing that, the greatest number and those the most important; the more so, in face of the cavilling criticism of the day. For whereas there have hitherto been good poets, each in his own branch, the critics now expect one man to surpass all others in their several lines of excellence.

In speaking of a tragedy as the same or different, the best test to take is the plot. Identity exists where the Complication and Unravelling are the same. Many poets tie the knot well, but unravel it ill. Both arts, however, should always be mastered.

Again, the poet should remember what has been often said, and not make an Epic structure into a Tragedy--by an Epic structure I mean one with a multiplicity of plots--as if, for instance, you were to make a tragedy out of the entire story of the Iliad. In the Epic poem, owing to its length, each part assumes its proper magnitude. In the drama the result is far from answering to the poet's expectation. The proof is that the poets who have dramatised the whole story of the Fall of Troy, instead of selecting portions, like Euripides; or who have taken the whole tale of Niobe, and not a part of her story, like Aeschylus, either fail utterly or meet with poor success on the stage. Even Agathon has been known to fail from this one defect. In his Reversals of the Situation, however, he shows a marvellous skill in the effort to hit the popular taste,--to produce a tragic effect that satisfies the moral sense. This effect is produced when the clever rogue, like Sisyphus, is outwitted, or the brave villain defeated. Such an event is probable in Agathon's sense of the word: 'it is probable,' he says, 'that many things should happen contrary to probability.'

The Chorus too should be regarded as one of the actors; it should be an integral part of the whole, and share in the action, in the manner not of Euripides but of Sophocles. As for the later poets, their choral songs pertain as little to the subject of the piece as to that of any other tragedy. They are, therefore, sung as mere interludes, a practice first begun by Agathon. Yet what difference is there between introducing such choral interludes, and transferring a speech, or even a whole act, from one play to another?

XIX

It remains to speak of Diction and Thought, the other parts of Tragedy having been already discussed. Concerning Thought, we may assume what is said in the Rhetoric, to which inquiry the subject more strictly belongs. Under Thought is included every effect which has to be produced by speech, the subdivisions being,-- proof and refutation; the excitation of the feelings, such as pity, fear, anger, and the like; the suggestion of importance or its opposite. Now, it is evident that the dramatic incidents must be treated from the same points of view as the dramatic speeches, when the object is to evoke the sense of pity, fear, importance, or probability. The only difference is, that the incidents should speak for themselves without verbal exposition; while the effects aimed at in speech should be produced by the speaker, and as a result of the speech. For what were the business of a speaker, if the Thought were revealed quite apart from what he says?

Next, as regards Diction. One branch of the inquiry treats of the Modes of Utterance. But this province of knowledge belongs to the art of Delivery and to the masters of that science. It includes, for instance,-- what is a command, a prayer, a statement, a threat, a question, an answer, and so forth. To know or not to know these things involves no serious censure upon the poet's art. For who can admit the fault imputed to Homer by Protagoras,--that in the words, 'Sing, goddess, of the wrath,' he gives a command under the idea that he utters a prayer? For to tell some one to do a thing or not to do it is, he says, a command. We may, therefore, pass this over as an inquiry that belongs to another art, not to poetry.

[Language in general includes the following parts:- Letter, Syllable, Connecting word, Noun, Verb, Inflexion or Case, Sentence or Phrase.

A Letter is an indivisible sound, yet not every such sound, but only one which can form part of a group of sounds. For even brutes utter indivisible sounds, none of which I call a letter. The sound I mean may be either a vowel, a semi-vowel, or a mute. A vowel is that which without impact of tongue or lip has an audible sound. A semi-vowel, that which with such impact has an audible sound, as S and R. A mute, that which with such impact has by itself no sound, but joined to a vowel sound becomes audible, as G and D. These are distinguished according to the form assumed by the mouth and the place where they are produced; according as they are aspirated or smooth, long or short; as they are acute, grave, or of an intermediate tone; which inquiry belongs in detail to the writers on metre.

A Syllable is a non-significant sound, composed of a mute and a vowel: for GR without A is a syllable, as also with A,--GRA. But the investigation of these differences belongs also to metrical science.

A Connecting word is a non-significant sound, which neither causes nor hinders the union of many sounds into one significant sound; it may be placed at either end or in the middle of a sentence. Or, a non- significant sound, which out of several sounds, each of them significant, is capable of forming one significant sound,--as {alpha mu theta iota}, {pi epsilon rho iota}, and the like. Or, a non-significant sound, which marks the beginning, end, or division of a sentence; such, however, that it cannot correctly stand by itself at the beginning of a sentence, as {mu epsilon nu}, {eta tau omicron iota}, {delta epsilon}.

A Noun is a composite significant sound, not marking time, of which no part is in itself significant: for in double or compound words we do not employ the separate parts as if each were in itself significant. Thus in Theodorus, 'god-given,' the {delta omega rho omicron nu} or 'gift' is not in itself significant.

A Verb is a composite significant sound, marking time, in which, as in the noun, no part is in itself significant. For 'man,' or 'white' does not express the idea of 'when'; but 'he walks,' or 'he has walked' does connote time, present or past.

Inflexion belongs both to the noun and verb, and expresses either the relation 'of,' 'to,' or the like; or that of number, whether one or many, as 'man' or 'men '; or the modes or tones in actual delivery, e.g. a question or a command. 'Did he go?' and 'go' are verbal inflexions of this kind.

A Sentence or Phrase is a composite significant sound, some at least of whose parts are in themselves significant; for not every such group of words consists of verbs and nouns--'the definition of man,' for example - -but it may dispense even with the verb. Still it will always have some significant part, as 'in walking,' or 'Cleon son of Cleon.' A sentence or phrase may form a unity in two ways,--either as signifying one thing, or as consisting of several parts linked together. Thus the Iliad is one by the linking together of parts, the definition of man by the unity of the thing signified.]

XXI

Words are of two kinds, simple and double. By simple I mean those composed of non-significant elements, such as {gamma eta}. By double or compound, those composed either of a significant and non-significant element (though within the whole word no element is significant), or of elements that are both significant. A word may likewise be triple, quadruple, or multiple in form, like so many Massilian expressions, e.g. 'Hermo-caico-xanthus who prayed to Father Zeus>.'

Every word is either current, or strange, or metaphorical, or ornamental, or newly-coined, or lengthened, or contracted, or altered.

By a current or proper word I mean one which is in general use among a people; by a strange word, one which is in use in another country. Plainly, therefore, the same word may be at once strange and current, but not in relation to the same people. The word {sigma iota gamma upsilon nu omicron nu}, 'lance,' is to the Cyprians a current term but to us a strange one.

Metaphor is the application of an alien name by transference either from genus to species, or from species to genus, or from species to species, or by analogy, that is, proportion. Thus from genus to species, as: 'There lies my ship'; for lying at anchor is a species of lying. From species to genus, as: 'Verily ten thousand noble deeds hath Odysseus wrought'; for ten thousand is a species of large number, and is here used for a large number generally. From species to species, as: 'With blade of bronze drew away the life,' and 'Cleft the water with the vessel of unyielding bronze.' Here {alpha rho upsilon rho alpha iota}, 'to draw away,' is used for {tau alpha mu epsilon iota nu}, 'to cleave,' and {tau alpha mu epsilon iota nu} again for {alpha rho upsilon alpha iota},--each being a species of taking away. Analogy or proportion is when the second term is to the first as the fourth to the third. We may then use the fourth for the second, or the second for the fourth. Sometimes too we qualify the metaphor by adding the term to which the proper word is relative. Thus the cup is to Dionysus as the shield to Ares. The cup may, therefore, be called 'the shield of Dionysus,' and the shield 'the cup of Ares.' Or, again, as old age is to life, so is evening to day. Evening may therefore be called 'the old age of the day,' and old age, 'the evening of life,' or, in the phrase of Empedocles, 'life's setting sun.' For some of the terms of the proportion there is at times no word in existence; still the metaphor may be used. For instance, to scatter seed is called sowing: but the action of the sun in scattering his rays is nameless. Still this process bears to the sun the same relation as sowing to the seed. Hence the expression of the poet 'sowing the god-created light.' There is another way in which this kind of metaphor may be employed. We may apply an alien term, and then deny of that term one of its proper attributes; as if we were to call the shield, not 'the cup of Ares,' but 'the wineless cup.'

<An ornamental word . . .>

A newly-coined word is one which has never been even in local use, but is adopted by the poet himself. Some such words there appear to be: as {epsilon rho nu upsilon gamma epsilon sigma}, 'sprouters,' for {kappa epsilon rho alpha tau alpha}, 'horns,' and {alpha rho eta tau eta rho}, 'supplicator,' for {iota epsilon rho epsilon upsilon sigma}, 'priest.'

A word is lengthened when its own vowel is exchanged for a longer one, or when a syllable is inserted. A word is contracted when some part of it is removed. Instances of lengthening are,--{pi omicron lambda eta omicron sigma} for {pi omicron lambda epsilon omega sigma}, and {Pi eta lambda eta iota alpha delta epsilon omega} for {Pi eta lambda epsilon iota delta omicron upsilon}: of contraction,--{kappa rho iota}, {delta omega}, and {omicron psi}, as in {mu iota alpha / gamma iota nu epsilon tau alpha iota / alpha mu phi omicron tau epislon rho omega nu / omicron psi}.

An altered word is one in which part of the ordinary form is left unchanged, and part is re-cast; as in {delta epsilon xi iota-tau epsilon rho omicron nu / kappa alpha tau alpha / mu alpha zeta omicron nu}, {delta epsilon xi iota tau epsilon rho omicron nu} is for {delta epsilon xi iota omicron nu}.

[Nouns in themselves are either masculine, feminine, or neuter. Masculine are such as end in {nu}, {rho}, {sigma}, or in some letter compounded with {sigma},--these being two, and {xi}. Feminine, such as end in vowels that are always long, namely {eta} and {omega}, and--of vowels that admit of lengthening--those in {alpha}. Thus the number of letters in which nouns masculine and feminine end is the same; for {psi} and {xi} are equivalent to endings in {sigma}. No noun ends in a mute or a vowel short by nature. Three only end in {iota},--{mu eta lambda iota}, {kappa omicron mu mu iota}, {pi epsilon pi epsilon rho iota}: five end in {upsilon}. Neuter nouns end in these two latter vowels; also in {nu} and {sigma}.]

XXII

The perfection of style is to be clear without being mean. The clearest style is that which uses only current or proper words; at the same time it is mean:-- witness the poetry of Cleophon and of Sthenelus. That diction, on the other hand, is lofty and raised above the commonplace which employs unusual words. By unusual, I mean strange (or rare) words, metaphorical, lengthened,--anything, in short, that differs from the normal idiom. Yet a style wholly composed of such words is either a riddle or a jargon; a riddle, if it consists of metaphors; a jargon, if it consists of strange (or rare) words. For the essence of a riddle is to express true facts under impossible combinations. Now this cannot be done by any arrangement of ordinary words, but by the use of metaphor it can. Such is the riddle:--'A man I saw who on another man had glued the bronze by aid of fire,' and others of the same kind. A diction that is made up of strange (or rare) terms is a jargon. A certain infusion, therefore, of these elements is necessary to style; for the strange (or rare) word, the metaphorical, the ornamental, and the other kinds above mentioned, will raise it above the commonplace and mean, while the use of proper words will make it perspicuous. But nothing contributes more to produce a clearness of diction that is remote from commonness than the lengthening, contraction, and alteration of words. For by deviating in exceptional cases from the normal idiom, the language will gain distinction; while, at the same time, the partial conformity with usage will give perspicuity. The critics, therefore, are in error who censure these licenses of speech, and hold the author up to ridicule. Thus Eucleides, the elder, declared that it would be an easy matter to be a poet if you might lengthen syllables at will. He caricatured the practice in the very form of his diction, as in the verse: '{Epsilon pi iota chi alpha rho eta nu / epsilon iota delta omicron nu / Mu alpha rho alpha theta omega nu alpha delta epsilon / Beta alpha delta iota zeta omicron nu tau alpha}, or, {omicron upsilon kappa / alpha nu / gamma / epsilon rho alpha mu epsilon nu omicron sigma / tau omicron nu / epsilon kappa epsilon iota nu omicron upsilon /epsilon lambda lambda epsilon beta omicron rho omicron nu}. To employ such license at all obtrusively is, no doubt, grotesque; but in any mode of poetic diction there must be moderation. Even metaphors, strange (or rare) words, or any similar forms of speech, would produce the like effect if used without propriety and with the express purpose of being ludicrous. How great a difference is made by the appropriate use of lengthening, may be seen in Epic poetry by the insertion of ordinary forms in the verse. So, again, if we take a strange (or rare) word, a metaphor, or any similar mode of expression, and replace it by the current or proper term, the truth of our observation will be manifest. For example Aeschylus and Euripides each composed the same iambic line. But the alteration of a single word by Euripides, who employed the rarer term instead of the ordinary one, makes one verse appear beautiful and the other trivial. Aeschylus in his Philoctetes says: {Phi alpha gamma epsilon delta alpha iota nu alpha / <delta> / eta / mu omicron upsilon / sigma alpha rho kappa alpha sigma / epsilon rho theta iota epsilon iota / pi omicron delta omicron sigma}.

Euripides substitutes {Theta omicron iota nu alpha tau alpha iota} 'feasts on' for {epsilon sigma theta iota epsilon iota} 'feeds on.' Again, in the line, {nu upsilon nu / delta epsilon / mu /epsilon omega nu / omicron lambda iota gamma iota gamma upsilon sigma / tau epsilon / kappa alpha iota / omicron upsilon tau iota delta alpha nu omicron sigma / kappa alpha iota / alpha epsilon iota kappa eta sigma, the difference will be felt if we substitute the common words, {nu upsilon nu / delta epsilon / mu / epsilon omega nu / mu iota kappa rho omicron sigma / tau epsilon / kappa alpha iota / alpha rho theta epsilon nu iota kappa omicron sigma / kappa alpha iota / alpha epsilon iota delta gamma sigma}. Or, if for the line, {delta iota phi rho omicron nu / alpha epsilon iota kappa epsilon lambda iota omicron nu / kappa alpha tau alpha theta epsilon iota sigma / omicron lambda iota gamma eta nu / tau epsilon / tau rho alpha pi epsilon iota sigma / omicron lambda iota gamma eta nu / tau epsilon / tau rho alpha pi epsilon zeta alpha nu),} We read, {delta iota phi rho omicron nu / mu omicron chi theta eta rho omicron nu / kappa alpha tau alpha theta epsilon iota sigma / mu iota kappa rho alpha nu / tau epsilon / tau rho alpha pi epsilon zeta alpha nu}.

Or, for {eta iota omicron nu epsilon sigma / beta omicron omicron omega rho iota nu, eta iota omicron nu epsilon sigma kappa rho alpha zeta omicron upsilon rho iota nu}

Again, Ariphrades ridiculed the tragedians for using phrases which no one would employ in ordinary speech: for example, {delta omega mu alpha tau omega nu / alpha pi omicron} instead of {alpha pi omicron / delta omega mu alpha tau omega nu}, {rho epsilon theta epsilon nu}, {epsilon gamma omega / delta epsilon / nu iota nu}, {Alpha chi iota lambda lambda epsilon omega sigma / pi epsilon rho iota} instead of (pi epsilon rho iota / 'Alpha chi iota lambda lambda epsilon omega sigma}, and the like. It is precisely because such phrases are not part of the current idiom that they give distinction to the style. This, however, he failed to see.

It is a great matter to observe propriety in these several modes of expression, as also in compound words, strange (or rare) words, and so forth. But the greatest thing by far is to have a command of metaphor. This alone cannot be imparted by another; it is the mark of genius, for to make good metaphors implies an eye for resemblances.

Of the various kinds of words, the compound are best adapted to Dithyrambs, rare words to heroic poetry, metaphors to iambic. In heroic poetry, indeed, all these varieties are serviceable. But in iambic verse, which reproduces, as far as may be, familiar speech, the most appropriate words are those which are found even in prose. These are,--the current or proper, the metaphorical, the ornamental.

Concerning Tragedy and imitation by means of action this may suffice.

XXIII

As to that poetic imitation which is narrative in form and employs a single metre, the plot manifestly ought, as in a tragedy, to be constructed on dramatic principles. It should have for its subject a single action, whole and complete, with a beginning, a middle, and an end. It will thus resemble a living organism in all its unity, and produce the pleasure proper to it. It will differ in structure from historical compositions, which of necessity present not a single action, but a single period, and all that happened within that period to one person or to many, little connected together as the events may be. For as the sea-fight at Salamis and the battle with the Carthaginians in Sicily took place at the same time, but did not tend to any one result, so in the sequence of events, one thing sometimes follows another, and yet no single result is thereby produced. Such is the practice, we may say, of most poets. Here again, then, as has been already observed, the transcendent excellence of Homer is manifest. He never attempts to make the whole war of Troy the subject of his poem, though that war had a beginning and an end. It would have been too vast a theme, and not easily embraced in a single view. If, again, he had kept it within moderate limits, it must have been over-complicated by the variety of the incidents. As it is, he detaches a single portion, and admits as episodes many events from the general story of the war--such as the Catalogue of the ships and others--thus diversifying the poem. All other poets take a single hero, a single period, or an action single indeed, but with a multiplicity of parts. Thus did the author of the Cypria and of the Little Iliad. For this reason the Iliad and the Odyssey each furnish the subject of one tragedy, or, at most, of two; while the Cypria supplies materials for many, and the Little Iliad for eight--the Award of the Arms, the Philoctetes, the Neoptolemus, the Eurypylus, the Mendicant Odysseus, the Laconian Women, the Fall of Ilium, the Departure of the Fleet.

XXIV

Again, Epic poetry must have as many kinds as Tragedy: it must be simple, or complex, or 'ethical,' or 'pathetic.' The parts also, with the exception of song and spectacle, are the same; for it requires Reversals of the Situation, Recognitions, and Scenes of Suffering. Moreover, the thoughts and the diction must be artistic. In all these respects Homer is our earliest and sufficient model. Indeed each of his poems has a twofold character. The Iliad is at once simple and 'pathetic,' and the Odyssey complex (for Recognition scenes run through it), and at the same time 'ethical.' Moreover, in diction and thought they are supreme.

Epic poetry differs from Tragedy in the scale on which it is constructed, and in its metre. As regards scale or length, we have already laid down an adequate limit:--the beginning and the end must be capable of being brought within a single view. This condition will be satisfied by poems on a smaller scale than the old epics, and answering in length to the group of tragedies presented at a single sitting.

Epic poetry has, however, a great--a special--capacity for enlarging its dimensions, and we can see the reason. In Tragedy we cannot imitate several lines of actions carried on at one and the same time; we must confine ourselves to the action on the stage and the part taken by the players. But in Epic poetry, owing to the narrative form, many events simultaneously transacted can be presented; and these, if relevant to the subject, add mass and dignity to the poem. The Epic has here an advantage, and one that conduces to grandeur of effect, to diverting the mind of the hearer, and relieving the story with varying episodes. For sameness of incident soon produces satiety, and makes tragedies fail on the stage.

As for the metre, the heroic measure has proved its fitness by the test of experience. If a narrative poem in any other metre or in many metres were now composed, it would be found incongruous. For of all measures the heroic is the stateliest and the most massive; and hence it most readily admits rare words and metaphors, which is another point in which the narrative form of imitation stands alone. On the other hand, the iambic and the trochaic tetrameter are stirring measures, the latter being akin to dancing, the former expressive of action. Still more absurd would it be to mix together different metres, as was done by Chaeremon. Hence no one has ever composed a poem on a great scale in any other than heroic verse. Nature herself, as we have said, teaches the choice of the proper measure.

Homer, admirable in all respects, has the special merit of being the only poet who rightly appreciates the part he should take himself. The poet should speak as little as possible in his own person, for it is not this that makes him an imitator. Other poets appear themselves upon the scene throughout, and imitate but little and rarely. Homer, after a few prefatory words, at once brings in a man, or woman, or other personage; none of them wanting in characteristic qualities, but each with a character of his own.

The element of the wonderful is required in Tragedy. The irrational, on which the wonderful depends for its chief effects, has wider scope in Epic poetry, because there the person acting is not seen. Thus, the pursuit of Hector would be ludicrous if placed upon the stage--the Greeks standing still and not joining in the pursuit, and Achilles waving them back. But in the Epic poem the absurdity passes unnoticed. Now the wonderful is pleasing: as may be inferred from the fact that every one tells a story with some addition of his own, knowing that his hearers like it. It is Homer who has chiefly taught other poets the art of telling lies skilfully. The secret of it lies in a fallacy, For, assuming that if one thing is or becomes, a second is or becomes, men imagine that, if the second is, the first likewise is or becomes. But this is a false inference. Hence, where the first thing is untrue, it is quite unnecessary, provided the second be true, to add that the first is or has become. For the mind, knowing the second to be true, falsely infers the truth of the first. There is an example of this in the Bath Scene of the Odyssey.

Accordingly, the poet should prefer probable impossibilities to improbable possibilities. The tragic plot must not be composed of irrational parts. Everything irrational should, if possible, be excluded; or, at all events, it should lie outside the action of the play (as, in the Oedipus, the hero's ignorance as to the manner of Laius' death); not within the drama,--as in the Electra, the messenger's account of the Pythian games; or, as in the Mysians, the man who has come from Tegea to Mysia and is still speechless. The plea that otherwise the plot would have been ruined, is ridiculous; such a plot should not in the first instance be constructed. But once the irrational has been introduced and an air of likelihood imparted to it, we must accept it in spite of the absurdity. Take even the irrational incidents in the Odyssey, where Odysseus is left upon the shore of Ithaca. How intolerable even these might have been would be apparent if an inferior poet were to treat the subject. As it is, the absurdity is veiled by the poetic charm with which the poet invests it.

The diction should be elaborated in the pauses of the action, where there is no expression of character or thought. For, conversely, character and thought are merely obscured by a diction that is over brilliant.

XXV

With respect to critical difficulties and their solutions, the number and nature of the sources from which they may be drawn may be thus exhibited.

The poet being an imitator, like a painter or any other artist, must of necessity imitate one of three objects,--things as they were or are, things as they are said or thought to be, or things as they ought to be. The vehicle of expression is language,--either current terms or, it may be, rare words or metaphors. There are also many modifications of language, which we concede to the poets. Add to this, that the standard of correctness is not the same in poetry and politics, any more than in poetry and any other art. Within the art of poetry itself there are two kinds of faults, those which touch its essence, and those which are accidental. If a poet has chosen to imitate something, <but has imitated it incorrectly> through want of capacity, the error is inherent in the poetry. But if the failure is due to a wrong choice if he has represented a horse as throwing out both his off legs at once, or introduced technical inaccuracies in medicine, for example, or in any other art the error is not essential to the poetry. These are the points of view from which we should consider and answer the objections raised by the critics.

First as to matters which concern the poet's own art. If he describes the impossible, he is guilty of an error; but the error may be justified, if the end of the art be thereby attained (the end being that already mentioned), if, that is, the effect of this or any other part of the poem is thus rendered more striking. A case in point is the pursuit of Hector. If, however, the end might have been as well, or better, attained without violating the special rules of the poetic art, the error is not justified: for every kind of error should, if possible, be avoided.

Again, does the error touch the essentials of the poetic art, or some accident of it? For example,--not to know that a hind has no horns is a less serious matter than to paint it inartistically.

Further, if it be objected that the description is not true to fact, the poet may perhaps reply,--'But the objects are as they ought to be': just as Sophocles said that he drew men as they ought to be; Euripides, as they are. In this way the objection may be met. If, however, the representation be of neither kind, the poet may answer,--This is how men say the thing is.' This applies to tales about the gods. It may well be that these stories are not higher than fact nor yet true to fact: they are, very possibly, what Xenophanes says of them. But anyhow, 'this is what is said.' Again, a description may be no better than the fact: 'still, it was the fact'; as in the passage about the arms: 'Upright upon their butt-ends stood the spears.' This was the custom then, as it now is among the Illyrians.

Again, in examining whether what has been said or done by some one is poetically right or not, we must not look merely to the particular act or saying, and ask whether it is poetically good or bad. We must also consider by whom it is said or done, to whom, when, by what means, or for what end; whether, for instance, it be to secure a greater good, or avert a greater evil.

Other difficulties may be resolved by due regard to the usage of language. We may note a rare word, as in {omicron upsilon rho eta alpha sigma / mu epsilon nu / pi rho omega tau omicron nu}, where the poet perhaps employs {omicron upsilon rho eta alpha sigma} not in the sense of mules, but of sentinels. So, again, of Dolon: 'ill-favoured indeed he was to look upon.' It is not meant that his body was ill-shaped, but that his face was ugly; for the Cretans use the word {epsilon upsilon epsilon iota delta epsilon sigma}, 'well-favoured,' to denote a fair face. Again, {zeta omega rho omicron tau epsilon rho omicron nu / delta epsilon / kappa epsilon rho alpha iota epsilon}, 'mix the drink livelier,' does not mean `mix it stronger' as for hard drinkers, but 'mix it quicker.'

Sometimes an expression is metaphorical, as 'Now all gods and men were sleeping through the night,'--while at the same time the poet says: 'Often indeed as he turned his gaze to the Trojan plain, he marvelled at the sound of flutes and pipes.' 'All' is here used metaphorically for 'many,' all being a species of many. So in the verse,--'alone she hath no part . . ,' {omicron iota eta}, 'alone,' is metaphorical; for the best known may be called the only one.

Again, the solution may depend upon accent or breathing. Thus Hippias of Thasos solved the difficulties in the lines,--{delta iota delta omicron mu epsilon nu (delta iota delta omicron mu epsilon nu) delta epsilon / omicron iota,} and { tau omicron / mu epsilon nu / omicron upsilon (omicron upsilon) kappa alpha tau alpha pi upsilon theta epsilon tau alpha iota / omicron mu beta rho omega}.

Or again, the question may be solved by punctuation, as in Empedocles,-- 'Of a sudden things became mortal that before had learnt to be immortal, and things unmixed before mixed.'

Or again, by ambiguity of meaning,--as {pi alpha rho omega chi eta kappa epsilon nu / delta epsilon / pi lambda epsilon omega / nu upsilon xi}, where the word {pi lambda epsilon omega} is ambiguous.

Or by the usage of language. Thus any mixed drink is called {omicron iota nu omicron sigma}, 'wine.' Hence Ganymede is said 'to pour the wine to Zeus,' though the gods do not drink wine. So too workers in iron are called {chi alpha lambda kappa epsilon alpha sigma}, or workers in bronze. This, however, may also be taken as a metaphor.

Again, when a word seems to involve some inconsistency of meaning, we should consider how many senses it may bear in the particular passage. For example: 'there was stayed the spear of bronze'--we should ask in how many ways we may take 'being checked there.' The true mode of interpretation is the precise opposite of what Glaucon mentions. Critics, he says, jump at certain groundless conclusions; they pass adverse judgment and then proceed to reason on it; and, assuming that the poet has said whatever they happen to think, find fault if a thing is inconsistent with their own fancy. The question about Icarius has been treated in this fashion. The critics imagine he was a Lacedaemonian. They think it strange, therefore, that Telemachus should not have met him when he went to Lacedaemon. But the Cephallenian story may perhaps be the true one. They allege that Odysseus took a wife from among themselves, and that her father was Icadius not Icarius. It is merely a mistake, then, that gives plausibility to the objection.

In general, the impossible must be justified by reference to artistic requirements, or to the higher reality, or to received opinion. With respect to the requirements of art, a probable impossibility is to be preferred to a thing improbable and yet possible. Again, it may be impossible that there should be men such as Zeuxis painted. 'Yes,' we say, 'but the impossible is the higher thing; for the ideal type must surpass the reality.' To justify the irrational, we appeal to what is commonly said to be. In addition to which, we urge that the irrational sometimes does not violate reason; just as 'it is probable that a thing may happen contrary to probability.'

Things that sound contradictory should be examined by the same rules as in dialectical refutation whether the same thing is meant, in the same relation, and in the same sense. We should therefore solve the question by reference to what the poet says himself, or to what is tacitly assumed by a person of intelligence.

The element of the irrational, and, similarly, depravity of character, are justly censured when there is no inner necessity for introducing them. Such is the irrational element in the introduction of Aegeus by Euripides and the badness of Menelaus in the Orestes.

Thus, there are five sources from which critical objections are drawn. Things are censured either as impossible, or irrational, or morally hurtful, or contradictory, or contrary to artistic correctness. The answers should be sought under the twelve heads above mentioned.

XXVI

The question may be raised whether the Epic or Tragic mode of imitation is the higher. If the more refined art is the higher, and the more refined in every case is that which appeals to the better sort of audience, the art which imitates anything and everything is manifestly most unrefined. The audience is supposed to be too dull to comprehend unless something of their own is thrown in by the performers, who therefore indulge in restless movements. Bad flute-players twist and twirl, if they have to represent 'the quoit-throw,' or hustle the coryphaeus when they perform the 'Scylla.' Tragedy, it is said, has this same defect. We may compare the opinion that the older actors entertained of their successors. Mynniscus used to call Callippides 'ape' on account of the extravagance of his action, and the same view was held of Pindarus. Tragic art, then, as a whole, stands to Epic in the same relation as the younger to the elder actors. So we are told that Epic poetry is addressed to a cultivated audience, who do not need gesture; Tragedy, to an inferior public. Being then unrefined, it is evidently the lower of the two.

Now, in the first place, this censure attaches not to the poetic but to the histrionic art; for gesticulation may be equally overdone in epic recitation, as by Sosi-stratus, or in lyrical competition, as by Mnasitheus the Opuntian. Next, all action is not to be condemned any more than all dancing--but only that of bad performers. Such was the fault found in Callippides, as also in others of our own day, who are censured for representing degraded women. Again, Tragedy like Epic poetry produces its effect even without action; it reveals its power by mere reading. If, then, in all other respects it is superior, this fault, we say, is not inherent in it.

And superior it is, because it has all the epic elements--it may even use the epic metre--with the music and spectacular effects as important accessories; and these produce the most vivid of pleasures. Further, it has vividness of impression in reading as well as in representation. Moreover, the art attains its end within narrower limits; for the concentrated effect is more pleasurable than one which is spread over a long time and so diluted. What, for example, would be the effect of the Oedipus of Sophocles, if it were cast into a form as long as the Iliad? Once more, the Epic imitation has less unity; as is shown by this, that any Epic poem will furnish subjects for several tragedies. Thus if the story adopted by the poet has a strict unity, it must either be concisely told and appear truncated; or, if it conform to the Epic canon of length, it must seem weak and watery. <Such length implies some loss of unity,> if, I mean, the poem is constructed out of several actions, like the Iliad and the Odyssey, which have many such parts, each with a certain magnitude of its own. Yet these poems are as perfect as possible in structure; each is, in the highest degree attainable, an imitation of a single action.

If, then, Tragedy is superior to Epic poetry in all these respects, and, moreover, fulfils its specific function better as an art for each art ought to produce, not any chance pleasure, but the pleasure proper to it, as already stated it plainly follows that Tragedy is the higher art, as attaining its end more perfectly.

Thus much may suffice concerning Tragic and Epic poetry in general; their several kinds and parts, with the number of each and their differences; the causes that make a poem good or bad; the objections of the critics and the answers to these objections.

Aristotle

Aristotle (/ˈærɪˌstɒtəl/;[1] Greek: Ἀριστοτέλης [aristotélɛːs], Aristotélēs; 384

– 322 BC)[2] was a Greek philosopher and scientist born in the Macedonian city of Stagira, Chalkidice, on the northern periphery of Classical Greece. His father, Nicomachus, died when Aristotle was a child, whereafter Proxenus of Atarneus became his guardian.[3] At eighteen, he joined Plato's Academy in Athens and remained there until the age of thirty-seven (c. 347 BC). His writings cover many subjects – including physics, biology, zoology, metaphysics, logic, ethics, aesthetics, poetry, theater, music, rhetoric, linguistics, politics and government – and constitute the first comprehensive system of Western philosophy. Shortly after Plato died, Aristotle left Athens and, at the request of Philip of Macedon, tutored Alexander the Great starting from 343 BC.[4] According to the Encyclopædia Britannica, "Aristotle was the first genuine scientist in history ... [and] every scientist is in his debt."[5]

Teaching Alexander the Great gave Aristotle many opportunities and an abundance of supplies. He established a library in the Lyceum which aided in the production of many of his hundreds of books. The fact that Aristotle was a pupil of Plato contributed to his former views of Platonism, but, following Plato's death, Aristotle immersed himself in empirical studies and shifted from Platonism to empiricism.[6] He believed all peoples' concepts and all of their knowledge was ultimately based on perception. Aristotle's views on natural sciences represent the groundwork underlying many of his works.

Aristotle's views on physical science profoundly shaped medieval scholarship. Their influence extended into the Renaissance and were not replaced systematically until the Enlightenment and theories such as classical mechanics. Some of Aristotle's zoological observations, such as on the hectocotyl (reproductive) arm of the octopus, were not confirmed or refuted until the 19th century. His works contain the earliest known formal study of logic, which was incorporated in the late 19th century into modern formal logic.

In metaphysics, Aristotelianism profoundly influenced Judeo-Islamic philosophical and theological thought during the Middle Ages and continues to influence Christian theology, especially the scholastic tradition of the Catholic Church. Aristotle was well known among medieval Muslim intellectuals and revered as "The First Teacher" (Arabic: المعلم الأول).

His ethics, though always influential, gained renewed interest with the modern advent of virtue ethics. All aspects of Aristotle's philosophy continue to be the object of active academic study today. Though Aristotle wrote many elegant treatises and dialogues – Cicero described his literary style as "a river of gold"[7] – it is thought that only around a third of his original output has survived.[8]

Aristotle, whose name means "the best purpose",[9] was born in 384 BC in Stagira, Chalcidice, about 55 km (34 miles) east of modern-day Thessaloniki.[10] His father Nicomachus was the personal physician to King Amyntas of Macedon. Although there is little information on Aristotle's childhood, he probably spent some time within the Macedonian palace, making his first connections with the Macedonian monarchy.[11]

At about the age of eighteen, Aristotle moved to Athens to continue his education at Plato's Academy. He remained there for nearly twenty years before leaving Athens in 348/47 BC. The traditional story about his departure records that he was disappointed with the Academy's direction after control passed to Plato's nephew Speusippus, although it is possible that he feared anti-Macedonian sentiments and left before Plato died.[12]

Aristotle then accompanied Xenocrates to the court of his friend Hermias of Atarneus in Asia Minor. There, he traveled with Theophrastus to the island of Lesbos, where together they researched the botany and zoology of the island. Aristotle married Pythias, either Hermias's adoptive daughter or niece. She bore him a daughter, whom they also named Pythias. Soon after Hermias' death, Aristotle was invited by Philip II of Macedon to become the tutor to his son Alexander in 343 BC.[4]

Aristotle was appointed as the head of the royal academy of Macedon. During that time he gave lessons not only to Alexander, but also to two other future kings: Ptolemy and Cassander.[13] Aristotle encouraged Alexander toward eastern conquest and his attitude towards Persia was unabashedly ethnocentric. In one famous example, he counsels Alexander to be "a leader to the Greeks and a despot to the barbarians, to look after the former as after friends and relatives, and to deal with the latter as with beasts or plants".[13]

By 335 BC, Artistotle had returned to Athens, establishing his own school there known as the Lyceum. Aristotle conducted courses at the school for the next twelve years. While in Athens, his wife Pythias died and Aristotle became involved with Herpyllis of Stagira, who bore him a son whom he named after his father, Nicomachus. According to the Suda, he also had an eromenos, Palaephatus of Abydus.[14]

This period in Athens, between 335 and 323 BC, is when Aristotle is believed to have composed many of his works.[4] He wrote many dialogues of which only fragments have survived. Those works that have survived are in treatise form and were not, for the most part, intended for widespread publication; they are generally thought to be lecture aids for his students. His most important treatises include Physics, Metaphysics, Nicomachean Ethics, Politics, De Anima (On the Soul) and Poetics.

Aristotle not only studied almost every subject possible at the time, but made significant contributions to most of them. In physical science, Aristotle studied anatomy, astronomy, embryology, geography, geology, meteorology, physics and zoology. In philosophy, he wrote on aesthetics, ethics, government, metaphysics, politics, economics, psychology, rhetoric and theology. He also studied education, foreign customs, literature and poetry. His combined works constitute a virtual encyclopedia of Greek knowledge.

Near the end of his life, Alexander and Aristotle became estranged over Alexander's relationship with Persia and Persians. A widespread tradition in antiquity suspected Aristotle of playing a role in Alexander's death, but there is little evidence.[15]

Following Alexander's death, anti-Macedonian sentiment in Athens was rekindled. In 322 BC, Eurymedon the Hierophant denounced Aristotle for not holding the gods in honor, prompting him to flee to his mother's family estate in Chalcis, explaining: "I will not allow the Athenians to sin twice against philosophy"[16][17] — a reference to Athens's prior trial and execution of Socrates. He died in Euboea of natural causes later that same year, having named his student Antipater as his chief executor and leaving a will in which he asked to be buried next to his wife.[18]

Charles Walston argues that the tomb of Aristotle is located on the sacred way between Chalcis and Eretria and to have contained two styluses, a pen, a signet-ring and some terra-cottas as well as what is supposed to be the earthly remains of Aristotle in the form of some skull fragments.[19]

In general, the details of the life of Aristotle are not well-established. The biographies of Aristotle written in ancient times are often speculative and historians only agree on a few salient points.[20]

Thought

Logic

With the Prior Analytics, Aristotle is credited with the earliest study of formal logic,[21] and his conception of it was the dominant form of Western logic until 19th century advances in mathematical logic.[22] Kant stated in the Critique of Pure Reason that Aristotle's theory of logic completely accounted for the core of deductive inference.

History

Aristotle "says that 'on the subject of reasoning' he 'had nothing else on an earlier date to speak of'".[23] However, Plato reports that syntax was devised before him, by Prodicus of Ceos, who was concerned by the correct use of words. Logic seems to have emerged from dialectics; the earlier philosophers made frequent use of concepts like reductio ad absurdum in their discussions, but never truly understood the logical implications. Even Plato had difficulties with logic; although he had a reasonable conception of a deductive system, he could never actually construct one, thus he relied instead on his dialectic.[24]

Plato believed that deduction would simply follow from premises, hence he focused on maintaining solid premises so that the conclusion would logically follow. Consequently, Plato realized that a method for obtaining conclusions would be most beneficial. He never succeeded in devising such a method, but his best attempt was published in his book Sophist, where he introduced his division method.[25]

Analytics and the Organon

What we today call Aristotelian logic, Aristotle himself would have labeled "analytics". The term "logic" he reserved to mean dialectics. Most of Aristotle's work is probably not in its original form, because it was most likely edited by students and later lecturers. The logical works of Aristotle were compiled into six books in about the early 1st century CE:

1.Categories
2.On Interpretation
3.Prior Analytics
4.Posterior Analytics
5.Topics
6.On Sophistical Refutations

The order of the books (or the teachings from which they are composed) is not certain, but this list was derived from analysis of Aristotle's writings. It goes from the basics, the analysis of simple terms in the Categories, the analysis of propositions and their elementary relations in On Interpretation, to the study of more complex forms, namely, syllogisms (in the Analytics) and dialectics (in the Topics and Sophistical Refutations). The first three treatises form the core of the logical theory stricto sensu: the grammar of the language of logic and the correct rules of reasoning. There is one volume of Aristotle's concerning logic not found in the Organon, namely the fourth book of Metaphysics.[24]

gestures to the earth, representing his belief in knowledge through empirical observation and experience, while holding a copy of his Nicomachean Ethics in his hand, whilst Plato gestures to the heavens, representing his belief in The Forms, while holding a copy of Timaeus

Like his teacher Plato, Aristotle's philosophy aims at the universal. Aristotle's ontology, however, finds the universal in particular things, which he calls the essence of things, while in Plato's ontology, the universal exists apart from particular things, and is related to them as their prototype or exemplar. For Aristotle, therefore, epistemology is based on the study of particular phenomena and rises to the knowledge of essences, while for Plato epistemology begins with knowledge of universal Forms (or ideas) and descends to knowledge of particular imitations of these. For Aristotle, "form" still refers to the unconditional basis of phenomena but is "instantiated" in a particular substance (see Universals and particulars, below). In a certain sense, Aristotle's method is both inductive and deductive, while Plato's is essentially deductive from a priori principles.[26]

In Aristotle's terminology, "natural philosophy" is a branch of philosophy examining the phenomena of the natural world, and includes fields that would be regarded today as physics, biology and other natural sciences. In modern times, the scope of philosophy has become limited to more generic or abstract inquiries, such as ethics and metaphysics, in which logic plays a major role. Today's philosophy tends to exclude empirical study of the natural world by means of the scientific method. In contrast, Aristotle's philosophical endeavors encompassed virtually all facets of intellectual inquiry.

In the larger sense of the word, Aristotle makes philosophy coextensive with reasoning, which he also would describe as "science". Note, however, that his use of the term science carries a different meaning than that covered by the term "scientific method". For Aristotle, "all science (dianoia) is either practical, poetical or theoretical" (Metaphysics 1025b25). By practical science, he means ethics and politics; by poetical science, he means the study of poetry and the other fine arts; by theoretical science, he means physics, mathematics and metaphysics.

If logic (or "analytics") is regarded as a study preliminary to philosophy, the divisions of Aristotelian philosophy would consist of: (1) Logic; (2) Theoretical Philosophy, including Metaphysics, Physics and Mathematics; (3) Practical Philosophy and (4) Poetical Philosophy.

In the period between his two stays in Athens, between his times at the Academy and the Lyceum, Aristotle conducted most of the scientific thinking and research for which he is renowned today. In fact, most of Aristotle's life was devoted to the study of the objects of natural science. Aristotle's metaphysics contains observations on the nature of numbers but he made no original contributions to mathematics. He did, however, perform original research in the natural sciences, e.g., botany, zoology, physics, astronomy, chemistry, meteorology, and several other sciences.

Aristotle's writings on science are largely qualitative, as opposed to quantitative. Beginning in the 16th century, scientists began applying mathematics to the physical sciences, and Aristotle's work in this area was deemed hopelessly inadequate. His failings were largely due to the absence of concepts like mass, velocity, force and temperature. He had a conception of speed and temperature, but no quantitative understanding of them, which was partly due to the absence of basic experimental devices, like clocks and thermometers.

His writings provide an account of many scientific observations, a mixture of precocious accuracy and curious errors. For example, in his History of Animals he claimed that human males have more teeth than females.[27] In a similar vein, John Philoponus, and later Galileo, showed by simple experiments that Aristotle's theory that a heavier object falls faster than a lighter object is incorrect.[28] On the other hand, Aristotle refuted Democritus's claim that the Milky Way was made up of "those stars which are shaded by the earth from the sun's rays," pointing out (correctly, even if such reasoning was bound to be dismissed for a long time) that, given "current astronomical demonstrations" that "the size of the sun is greater than that of the earth and the distance of the stars from the earth many times greater than that of the sun, then ... the sun shines on all the stars and the earth screens none of them."[29]

In places, Aristotle goes too far in deriving 'laws of the universe' from simple observation and over-stretched reason. Today's scientific method assumes that such thinking without sufficient facts is ineffective, and that discerning the validity of one's hypothesis requires far more rigorous experimentation than that which Aristotle used to support his laws.

Aristotle also had some scientific blind spots. He posited a geocentric cosmology that we may discern in selections of the Metaphysics, which was widely accepted up until the 16th century. From the 3rd century to the 16th century, the dominant view held that the Earth was the rotational center of the universe.

Because he was perhaps the philosopher most respected by European thinkers during and after the Renaissance, these thinkers often took Aristotle's erroneous positions as given, which held back science in this epoch.[30] However, Aristotle's scientific shortcomings should not mislead one into forgetting his great advances in the many scientific fields. For instance, he founded logic as a formal science and created foundations to biology that were not superseded for two millennia. Moreover, he introduced the fundamental notion that nature is composed of things that change and that studying such changes can provide useful knowledge of underlying constants.

Geology

He [Aristotle] refers to many examples of changes now constantly going on, and insists emphatically on the great results which they must produce in the lapse of ages. He instances particular cases of lakes that had dried up, and deserts that had at length become watered by rivers and fertilized. He points to the growth of the Nilotic delta since the time of Homer, to the shallowing of the Palus Maeotis within sixty years from his own time ... He alludes ... to the upheaving of one of the Eolian islands, previous to a volcanic eruption. The changes of the earth, he says, are so slow in comparison to the duration of our lives, that they are overlooked; and the migrations of people after great catastrophes, and their removal to other regions, cause the event to be forgotten.

He says [12th chapter of his Meteorics] 'the distribution of land and sea in particular regions does not endure throughout all time, but it becomes sea in those parts where it was land, and again it becomes land where it was sea, and there is reason for thinking that these changes take place according to a certain system, and within a certain period.' The concluding observation is as follows: 'As time never fails, and the universe is eternal, neither the Tanais, nor the Nile, can have flowed for ever. The places where they rise were once dry, and there is a limit to their operations, but there is none to time. So also of all other rivers; they spring up and they perish; and the sea also continually deserts some lands and invades others The same tracts, therefore, of the earth are not some always sea, and others always continents, but every thing changes in the course of time.'[31]

Physics

Five elements

Aristotle proposed a fifth element, aether, in addition to the four proposed earlier by Empedocles.

Earth, which is cold and dry; this corresponds to the modern idea of a solid.

Water, which is cold and wet; this corresponds to the modern idea of a liquid.

Air, which is hot and wet; this corresponds to the modern idea of a gas.

Fire, which is hot and dry; this corresponds to the modern ideas of plasma and heat.

Aether, which is the divine substance that makes up the heavenly spheres and heavenly bodies (stars and planets).

Each of the four earthly elements has its natural place. All that is earthly tends toward the center of the universe, i.e., the center of the Earth. Water tends toward a sphere surrounding the center. Air tends toward a sphere surrounding the water sphere. Fire tends toward the lunar sphere (in which the Moon orbits). When elements are moved out of their natural place, they naturally move back towards it. This is "natural motion"—motion requiring no extrinsic cause. So, for example, in water, earthy bodies sink while air bubbles rise up; in air, rain falls and flame rises. Outside all the other spheres, the heavenly, fifth element, manifested in the stars and planets, moves in the perfection of circles.

Motion

Aristotle defined motion as the actuality of a potentiality as such.[32] Aquinas suggested that the passage be understood literally; that motion can indeed be understood as the active fulfillment of a potential, as a transition toward a potentially possible state. Because actuality and potentiality are normally opposites in Aristotle, other commentators either suggest that the wording which has come down to us is erroneous, or that the addition of the "as such" to the definition is critical to understanding it.[33]

Causality, the four causes

Aristotle suggested that the reason for anything coming about can be attributed to four different types of simultaneously active causal factors:
Material cause describes the material out of which something is composed. Thus the material cause of a table is wood, and the material cause of a car is rubber and steel. It is not about action. It does not mean one domino knocks over another domino.
The formal cause is its form, i.e., the arrangement of that matter. It tells us what a thing is, that any thing is determined by the definition, form, pattern, essence, whole, synthesis or archetype. It embraces the account of causes in terms of fundamental principles or general laws, as the whole (i.e.,

macrostructure) is the cause of its parts, a relationship known as the whole-part causation. Plainly put, the formal cause is the idea existing in the first place as exemplar in the mind of the sculptor, and in the second place as intrinsic, determining cause, embodied in the matter. Formal cause could only refer to the essential quality of causation. A simple example of the formal cause is the mental image or idea that allows an artist, architect, or engineer to create his drawings.

The efficient cause is "the primary source", or that from which the change under consideration proceeds. It identifies 'what makes of what is made and what causes change of what is changed' and so suggests all sorts of agents, nonliving or living, acting as the sources of change or movement or rest. Representing the current understanding of causality as the relation of cause and effect, this covers the modern definitions of "cause" as either the agent or agency or particular events or states of affairs. So, take the two dominoes, this time of equal weighting, the first is knocked over causing the second also to fall over.

The final cause is its purpose, or that for the sake of which a thing exists or is done, including both purposeful and instrumental actions and activities. The final cause or teleos is the purpose or function that something is supposed to serve. This covers modern ideas of motivating causes, such as volition, need, desire, ethics, or spiritual beliefs.

Additionally, things can be causes of one another, causing each other reciprocally, as hard work causes fitness and vice versa, although not in the same way or function, the one is as the beginning of change, the other as the goal. (Thus Aristotle first suggested a reciprocal or circular causality as a relation of mutual dependence or influence of cause upon effect). Moreover, Aristotle indicated that the same thing can be the cause of contrary effects; its presence and absence may result in different outcomes. Simply it is the goal or purpose that brings about an event. Our two dominoes require someone or something to intentionally knock over the first domino, because it cannot fall of its own accord.

Aristotle marked two modes of causation: proper (prior) causation and accidental (chance) causation. All causes, proper and incidental, can be spoken as potential or as actual, particular or generic. The same language refers to the effects of causes, so that generic effects assigned to generic causes, particular effects to particular causes, operating causes to actual effects. Essentially, causality does not suggest a temporal relation between the cause and the effect.

Optics

Aristotle held more accurate theories on some optical concepts than other philosophers of his day. The second oldest written evidence of a camera obscura (after Mozi c. 400 BC) can be found in Aristotle's documentation of such a device in 350 BC in Problemata. Aristotle's apparatus contained a dark chamber that had a single small hole, or aperture, to allow for sunlight to enter. Aristotle used the device to make observations of the sun and noted that no matter what shape the hole was, the sun would still be correctly displayed as a round object. In modern cameras, this is analogous to the diaphragm. Aristotle also made the observation that when the distance between the aperture and the surface with the image increased, the image was magnified.[34]

Chance and spontaneity

According to Aristotle, spontaneity and chance are causes of some things, distinguishable from other types of cause. Chance as an incidental cause lies in the realm of accidental things. It is "from what is spontaneous" (but note that what is spontaneous does not come from chance). For a better understanding of Aristotle's conception of "chance" it might be better to think of "coincidence": Something takes place by chance if a person sets out with the intent of having one thing take place, but with the result of another thing (not intended) taking place.

For example: A person seeks donations. That person may find another person willing to donate a substantial sum. However, if the person seeking the donations met the person donating, not for the purpose of collecting donations, but for some other purpose, Aristotle would call the collecting of the donation by that particular donator a result of chance. It must be unusual that something happens by chance. In other words, if something happens all or most of the time, we cannot say that it is by chance.

There is also more specific kind of chance, which Aristotle names "luck", that can only apply to human beings, because it is in the sphere of moral actions. According to Aristotle, luck must involve choice (and thus deliberation), and only humans are capable of deliberation and choice. "What is not capable of action cannot do anything by chance".[35]

Metaphysics

Aristotle defines metaphysics as "the knowledge of immaterial being," or of "being in the highest degree of abstraction." He refers to metaphysics as "first philosophy", as well as "the theologic science."

Substance, potentiality and actuality

Aristotle examines the concepts of substance and essence (ousia) in his Metaphysics (Book VII), and he concludes that a particular substance is a combination of both matter and form. In book VIII, he distinguishes the matter of the substance as the substratum, or the stuff of which it is composed. For example, the matter of a house is the bricks, stones, timbers etc., or whatever constitutes the potential house, while the form of the substance is the actual house, namely 'covering for bodies and chattels' or any other differentia (see also predicables) that let us define something as a house. The formula that gives the components is the account of the matter, and the formula that gives the differentia is the account of the form.[36]

With regard to the change (kinesis) and its causes now, as he defines in his Physics and On Generation and Corruption 319b–320a, he distinguishes the coming to be from:

1.growth and diminution, which is change in quantity;

2.locomotion, which is change in space; and

3.alteration, which is change in quality.

The coming to be is a change where nothing persists of which the resultant is a property. In that particular change he introduces the concept of potentiality (dynamis) and actuality (entelecheia) in association with the matter and the form.

Referring to potentiality, this is what a thing is capable of doing, or being acted upon, if the conditions are right and it is not prevented by something else. For example, the seed of a plant in the soil is potentially (dynamei) plant, and if is not prevented by something, it will become a plant. Potentially beings can either 'act' (poiein) or 'be acted upon' (paschein), which can be either innate or learned. For example, the eyes possess the potentiality of sight (innate – being acted upon), while the capability of playing the flute can be possessed by learning (exercise – acting).

Actuality is the fulfillment of the end of the potentiality. Because the end (telos) is the principle of every change, and for the sake of the end exists potentiality, therefore actuality is the end. Referring then to our previous example, we could say that an actuality is when a plant does one of the activities that plants do.

"For that for the sake of which a thing is, is its principle, and the becoming is for the sake of the end; and the actuality is the end, and it is for the sake of this that the potentiality is acquired. For animals do not see in order that they may have sight, but they have sight that they may see."[37]

In summary, the matter used to make a house has potentiality to be a house and both the activity of building and the form of the final house are actualities, which is also a final cause or end. Then Aristotle proceeds and concludes that the actuality is prior to potentiality in formula, in time and in substantiality.

With this definition of the particular substance (i.e., matter and form), Aristotle tries to solve the problem of the unity of the beings, for example, "what is it that makes a man one"? Since, according to Plato there are two Ideas: animal and biped, how then is man a unity? However, according to Aristotle, the potential being (matter) and the actual one (form) are one and the same thing.[38]

Universals and particulars

Aristotle's predecessor, Plato, argued that all things have a universal form, which could be either a property, or a relation to other things. When we look at an apple, for example, we see an apple, and we can also analyze a form of an apple. In this distinction, there is a particular apple and a universal form of an apple. Moreover, we can place an apple next to a book, so that we can speak of both the book and apple as being next to each other.

Plato argued that there are some universal forms that are not a part of particular things. For example, it is possible that there is no particular good in existence, but "good" is still a proper universal form. Bertrand Russell is a 20th-century philosopher who agreed with Plato on the existence of "uninstantiated universals".

Aristotle disagreed with Plato on this point, arguing that all universals are instantiated. Aristotle argued that there are no universals that are unattached to existing things. According to Aristotle, if a universal exists, either as a particular or a relation, then there must have been, must be currently, or must be in the future, something on which the universal can be predicated. Consequently, according to Aristotle, if it is not the case that some universal can be predicated to an object that exists at some period of time, then it does not exist.

In addition, Aristotle disagreed with Plato about the location of universals. As Plato spoke of the world of the forms, a location where all universal forms subsist, Aristotle maintained that universals exist within each thing on which each universal is predicated. So, according to Aristotle, the form of apple exists within each apple, rather than in the world of the forms.

Biology and medicine

In Aristotelian science, especially in biology, things he saw himself have stood the test of time better than his retelling of the reports of others, which contain error and superstition. He dissected animals but not humans; his ideas on how the human body works have been almost entirely superseded.

Empirical research program

Aristotle is the earliest natural historian whose work has survived in some detail. Aristotle certainly did research on the natural history of Lesbos, and the surrounding seas and neighbouring areas. The works that reflect this research, such as History of Animals, Generation of Animals, and Parts of Animals, contain some observations and interpretations, along with sundry myths and mistakes. The most striking passages are about the sea-life visible from observation on Lesbos and available from the catches of fishermen. His observations on catfish, electric fish (Torpedo) and angler-fish are detailed, as is his writing on cephalopods, namely, Octopus, Sepia (cuttlefish) and the paper nautilus (Argonauta argo). His description of the hectocotyl arm, used in sexual reproduction, was widely disbelieved until its rediscovery in the 19th century. He separated the aquatic mammals from fish, and knew that sharks and rays were part of the group he called Selachē (selachians).[39]

Another good example of his methods comes from the Generation of Animals in which Aristotle describes breaking open fertilized chicken eggs at intervals to observe when visible organs were generated.

He gave accurate descriptions of ruminants' four-chambered fore-stomachs, and of the ovoviviparous embryological development of the hound shark Mustelus mustelus.[40]

Classification of living things

Aristotle distinguished about 500 species of birds, mammals and fishes.[41][42] His classification of living things contains some elements which still existed in the 19th century. What the modern zoologist would call vertebrates and invertebrates, Aristotle called 'animals with blood' and 'animals without blood' (he did not know that complex invertebrates do make use of hemoglobin, but of a different kind from vertebrates). Animals with blood were divided into live-bearing (mammals), and egg-bearing (birds and fish). Invertebrates ('animals without blood') are insects, crustacea (divided into non-shelled – cephalopods – and shelled) and testacea (molluscs). In some respects, this incomplete classification is better than that of Linnaeus, who crowded the invertebrata together into two groups, Insecta and Vermes (worms).

For Charles Singer, "Nothing is more remarkable than [Aristotle's] efforts to [exhibit] the relationships of living things as a scala naturae"[39] Aristotle's History of Animals classified organisms in relation to a hierarchical "Ladder of Life" (scala naturae or Great Chain of Being), placing them according to complexity of structure and function so that higher organisms showed greater vitality and ability to move.[43]

Aristotle believed that intellectual purposes, i.e., final causes, guided all natural processes. Such a teleological view gave Aristotle cause to justify his observed data as an expression of formal design. Noting that "no animal has, at the same time, both tusks and horns," and "a single-hooved animal with two horns I have never seen," Aristotle suggested that Nature, giving no animal both horns and tusks, was staving off vanity, and giving creatures faculties only to such a degree as they are necessary. Noting that ruminants had multiple stomachs and weak teeth, he supposed the first was to compensate for the latter, with Nature trying to preserve a type of balance.[44]

In a similar fashion, Aristotle believed that creatures were arranged in a graded scale of perfection rising from plants on up to man, the scala naturae.[45] His system had eleven grades, arranged according "to the degree to which they are infected with potentiality", expressed in their form at birth. The highest animals laid warm and wet creatures alive, the lowest bore theirs cold, dry, and in thick eggs.

Aristotle also held that the level of a creature's perfection was reflected in its form, but not preordained by that form. Ideas like this, and his ideas about souls, are not regarded as science at all in modern times.

He placed emphasis on the type(s) of soul an organism possessed, asserting that plants possess a vegetative soul, responsible for reproduction and growth, animals a vegetative and a sensitive soul, responsible for mobility and sensation, and humans a vegetative, a sensitive, and a rational soul, capable of thought and reflection.[46]

Aristotle, in contrast to earlier philosophers, but in accordance with the Egyptians, placed the rational soul in the heart, rather than the brain.[47] Notable is Aristotle's division of sensation and thought, which generally went against previous philosophers, with the exception of Alcmaeon.[48]

Successor: Theophrastus

Aristotle's successor at the Lyceum, Theophrastus, wrote a series of books on botany—the History of Plants—which survived as the most important contribution of antiquity to botany, even into the Middle Ages. Many of Theophrastus' names survive into modern times, such as carpos for fruit, and pericarpion for seed vessel.

Rather than focus on formal causes, as Aristotle did, Theophrastus suggested a mechanistic scheme, drawing analogies between natural and artificial processes, and relying on Aristotle's concept of the efficient cause. Theophrastus also recognized the role of sex in the reproduction of some higher plants, though this last discovery was lost in later ages.[49]

Influence on Hellenistic medicine

After Theophrastus, the Lyceum failed to produce any original work. Though interest in Aristotle's ideas survived, they were generally taken unquestioningly.[50] It is not until the age of Alexandria under the Ptolemies that advances in biology can be again found.

The first medical teacher at Alexandria, Herophilus of Chalcedon, corrected Aristotle, placing intelligence in the brain, and connected the nervous system to motion and sensation. Herophilus also distinguished between veins and arteries, noting that the latter pulse while the former do not.[51] Though a few ancient atomists such as Lucretius challenged the teleological viewpoint of Aristotelian ideas about life, teleology (and after the rise of Christianity, natural theology) would remain central to biological thought essentially until the 18th and 19th centuries. Ernst Mayr claimed that there was "nothing of any real consequence in biology after Lucretius and Galen until the Renaissance."[52] Aristotle's ideas of natural history and medicine survived, but they were generally taken unquestioningly.[53]

Psychology

Aristotle's psychology, given in his treatise On the Soul (peri psyche, often known by its Latin title De Anima), posits three kinds of soul ("psyches"): the vegetative soul, the sensitive soul, and the rational soul. Humans have a rational soul. This kind of soul is capable of the same powers as the other kinds: Like the vegetative soul it can grow and nourish itself; like the sensitive soul it can experience sensations and move locally. The unique part of the human, rational soul is its ability to receive forms of other things and compare them.

For Aristotle, the soul (psyche) was a simpler concept than it is for us today. By soul he simply meant the form of a living being. Because all beings are composites of form and matter, the form of living beings is that which endows them with what is specific to living beings, e.g. the ability to initiate movement (or in the case of plants, growth and chemical transformations, which Aristotle considers types of movement).[54]

Memory

According to Aristotle, memory is the ability to hold a perceived experience in your mind and to have the ability to distinguish between the internal "appearance" and an occurrence in the past.[55] In other words, a memory is a mental picture (phantasm) in which Aristotle defines in De Anima, as an appearance which is imprinted on the part of the body that forms a memory. Aristotle believed an "imprint" becomes impressed on a semi-fluid bodily organ that undergoes several changes in order to make a memory. A memory occurs when a stimuli is too complex that the nervous system (semi-fluid bodily organ) cannot receive all the impressions at once. These changes are the same as those involved in the operations of sensation, common sense, and thinking .[56] The mental picture imprinted on the bodily organ is the final product of the entire process of sense perception. It does not matter if the experience was seen or heard, every experience ends up as a mental image in memory [57]

Aristotle uses the word "memory" for two basic abilities. First, the actual retaining of the experience in the mnemonic "imprint" that can develop from sensation. Second, the intellectual anxiety that comes with the "imprint" due to being impressed at a particular time and processing specific contents. These abilities can be explained as memory is neither sensation nor thinking because is arises only after a lapse of time. Therefore, memory is of the past, [58] prediction is of the future, and sensation is of the present. The retrieval of our "imprints" cannot be performed suddenly. A transitional channel is needed and located in our past experiences, both for our previous experience and present experience.

Aristotle proposed that slow-witted people have good memory because the fluids in their brain do not wash away their memory organ used to imprint experiences and so the "imprint" can easily continue. However, they cannot be too slow or the hardened surface of the organ will not receive new "imprints". He believed the young and the old do not properly develop an "imprint". Young people undergo rapid changes as they develop, while the elderly's organs are beginning to decay, thus stunting new "imprints". Likewise, people who are too quick-witted are similar to the young and the image cannot be fixed because of the rapid changes of their organ. Because intellectual functions are not involved in memory, memories belong to some animals too, but only those in which have perception of time.

Recollection

Because Aristotle believes people receive all kinds of sense perceptions and people perceive them as images or "imprints", people are continually weaving together new "imprints" of things they experience. In order to search for these "imprints", people search the memory itself.[59] Within the memory, if one experience is offered instead of a specific memory, that person will reject this experience until they find what they are looking for. Recollection occurs when one experience naturally follows another. If the chain of "images" is needed, one memory will stimulate the other. If the chain of "images" is not needed, but expected, then it will only stimulate the other memory in most instances. When people recall experiences, they stimulate certain previous experiences until they have stimulated the one that was needed.[60]

Recollection is the self-directed activity of retrieving the information stored in a memory "imprint" after some time has passed. Retrieval of stored information is dependent on the scope of mnemonic capabilities of a being (human or animal) and the abilities the human or animal possesses .[61] Only humans will remember "imprints" of intellectual activity, such as numbers and words. Animals that have perception of time will be able to retrieve memories of their past observations. Remembering involves only perception of the things remembered and of the time passed. Recollection of an "imprint" is when the present experiences a person remembers are similar with elements corresponding in character and arrangement of past sensory experiences. When an "imprint" is recalled, it may bring forth a large group of related "imprints".[62]

Aristotle believed the chain of thought, which ends in recollection of certain "imprints", was connected systematically in three sorts of relationships: similarity, contrast, and contiguity. These three laws make up his Laws of Association. Aristotle believed that past experiences are hidden within our mind. A force operates to awaken the hidden material to bring up the actual experience. According to Aristotle, association is the power innate in a mental state, which operates upon the unexpressed remains of former experiences, allowing them to rise and be recalled.[63]

Dreams

Sleep

Before understanding Aristotle's take on dreams, first his idea of sleep must be examined. Aristotle gives an account of his explanation of sleep in On Sleep and Wakefulness.[64] Sleep takes place as a result of overuse of the senses[65] or of digestion,[64] so it is vital to the body, including the senses, so it can be revitalized.[65] While a person is asleep, the critical activities, which include thinking, sensing, recalling and remembering, do not function as they do during wakefulness.[65] Since a person cannot sense during sleep they can also not have a desire, which is the result of a sensation.[65] However, the senses are able to work during sleep,[65] albeit differently than when a person is awake because during sleep a person can still have sensory experiences.[64] Also, all of the senses are not inactive during sleep, only the ones that are weary.[65]

Theory of dreams

Dreams do not involve actually sensing a stimulus because, as discussed, the senses do not work as they normally do during sleep.[65] In dreams, sensation is still involved, but in an altered manner than when awake.[65] Aristotle explains the phenomenon that occurs when a person stares at a moving stimulus such as the waves in a body of water.[64] When they look away from that stimulus, the next thing they look at appears to be moving in a wave like motion. When a person perceives a stimulus and the stimulus is no longer the focus of their attention, it leaves an impression.[64] When the body is awake and the senses are functioning properly, a person constantly encounters new stimuli to sense and so the impressions left from previously perceived stimuli become irrelevant.[65] However, during sleep the impressions stimuli made throughout the day become noticed because there are not new sensory experiences to distract from these impressions that were made.[64] So, dreams result from these lasting impressions. Since impressions are all that are left and not the exact stimuli, dreams will not resemble the actual experience that occurred when awake.[66]

During sleep, a person is in an altered state of mind.[64] Aristotle compares a sleeping person to a person who is overtaken by strong feelings toward a stimulus.[64] For example, a person who has a strong infatuation with someone may begin to think they see that person everywhere because they are so overtaken by their feelings.[64] When a person is asleep, their senses are not acting as they do when they are awake and this results in them thinking like a person who is influenced by strong feelings.[64] Since a person sleeping is in this suggestible state, they become easily deceived by what appears in their dreams.[64]

When asleep, a person is unable to make judgments as they do when they are awake[64] Due to the senses not functioning normally during sleep, they are unable to help a person judge what is happening in their dream.[64] This in turn leads the person to believe the dream is real.[64] Dreams may be absurd in nature but the senses are not able to discern whether they are real or not.[64] So, the dreamer is left to accept the dream because they lack the choice to judge it.

One component of Aristotle's theory of dreams introduces ideas that are contradictory to previously held beliefs.[67] He claimed that dreams are not foretelling and that they are not sent by a divine being.[67] Aristotle reasoned that instances in which dreams do resemble future events are happenstances not divinations.[67] These ideas were contradictory to what had been believed about dreams, but at the time in which he introduced these ideas more thinkers were beginning to give naturalistic as opposed to supernatural explanations to phenomena.[67]

Aristotle also includes in his theory of dreams what constitutes a dream and what does not. He claimed that a dream is first established by the fact that the person is asleep when they experience it.[66] If a person had an image appear for a moment after waking up or if they see something in the dark it is not considered a dream because they were awake when it occurred.[66] Secondly, any sensory experience that actually occurs while a person is asleep and is perceived by the person while asleep does not qualify as part of a dream.[66] For example, if, while a person is sleeping, a door shuts and in their dream they hear a door is shut, Aristotle argues that this sensory experience is not part of the dream.[66] The actual sensory experience is perceived by the senses, the fact that it occurred while the person was asleep does not make it part of the dream.[66] Lastly, the images of dreams must be a result of lasting impressions of sensory experiences had when awake.[66]

Practical philosophy

Ethics

Aristotle considered ethics to be a practical rather than theoretical study, i.e., one aimed at becoming good and doing good rather than knowing for its own sake. He wrote several treatises on ethics, including most notably, the Nicomachean Ethics.

Aristotle taught that virtue has to do with the proper function (ergon) of a thing. An eye is only a good eye in so much as it can see, because the proper function of an eye is sight. Aristotle reasoned that humans must have a function specific to humans, and that this function must be an activity of the psuchē (normally translated as soul) in accordance with reason (logos). Aristotle identified such an optimum activity of the soul as the aim of all human deliberate action, eudaimonia, generally translated as "happiness" or sometimes "well being". To have the potential of ever being happy in this way necessarily requires a good character (ēthikē aretē), often translated as moral (or ethical) virtue (or excellence).[68]

Aristotle taught that to achieve a virtuous and potentially happy character requires a first stage of having the fortune to be habituated not deliberately, but by teachers, and experience, leading to a later stage in which one consciously chooses to do the best things. When the best people come to live life this way their practical wisdom (phronesis) and their intellect (nous) can develop with each other towards the highest possible human virtue, the wisdom of an accomplished theoretical or speculative thinker, or in other words, a philosopher.[69]

Politics

In addition to his works on ethics, which address the individual, Aristotle addressed the city in his work titled Politics. Aristotle considered the city to be a natural community. Moreover, he considered the city to be prior in importance to the family which in turn is prior to the individual, "for the whole must of necessity be prior to the part".[70] He also famously stated that "man is by nature a political animal". Aristotle conceived of politics as being like an organism rather than like a machine, and as a collection of parts none of which can exist without the others. Aristotle's conception of the city is organic, and he is considered one of the first to conceive of the city in this manner.[71]

The common modern understanding of a political community as a modern state is quite different from Aristotle's understanding. Although he was aware of the existence and potential of larger empires, the natural community according to Aristotle was the city (polis) which functions as a political "community" or "partnership" (koinōnia). The aim of the city is not just to avoid injustice or for economic stability, but rather to allow at least some citizens the possibility to live a good life, and to perform beautiful acts: "The political partnership must be regarded, therefore, as being for the sake of noble actions, not for the sake of living together." This is distinguished from modern approaches, beginning with social contract theory, according to which individuals leave the state of nature because of "fear of violent death" or its "inconveniences."[72]

For we all agree that the most excellent man should rule, i.e., the supreme by nature, and that the law rules and alone is authoritative; but the law is a kind of intelligence, i.e. a discourse based on intelligence. And again, what standard do we have, what criterion of good things, that is more precise than the intelligent man? For all that this man will choose, if the choice is based on his knowledge, are good things and their contraries are bad. And since everybody chooses most of all what conforms to their own proper dispositions (a just man choosing to live justly, a man with bravery to live bravely, likewise a self-controlled man to live with self-control), it is clear that the intelligent man will choose most of all to be intelligent; for this is the function of that capacity. Hence it's evident that, according to the most authoritative judgment, intelligence is supreme among goods.

Rhetoric and poetics

Aristotle considered epic poetry, tragedy, comedy, dithyrambic poetry and music to be imitative, each varying in imitation by medium, object, and manner.[74] For example, music imitates with the media of rhythm and harmony, whereas dance imitates with rhythm alone, and poetry with language. The forms also differ in their object of imitation. Comedy, for instance, is a dramatic imitation of men worse than average; whereas tragedy imitates men slightly better than average. Lastly, the forms differ in their manner of imitation – through narrative or character, through change or no change, and through drama or no drama.[75] Aristotle believed that imitation is natural to mankind and constitutes one of mankind's advantages over animals.[76]

While it is believed that Aristotle's Poetics comprised two books – one on comedy and one on tragedy – only the portion that focuses on tragedy has survived. Aristotle taught that tragedy is composed of six elements: plot-structure, character, style, thought, spectacle, and lyric poetry.[77] The characters in a tragedy are merely a means of driving the story; and the plot, not the characters, is the chief focus of tragedy. Tragedy is the imitation of action arousing pity and fear, and is meant to effect the catharsis of those same emotions. Aristotle concludes Poetics with a discussion on which, if either, is superior: epic or tragic mimesis. He suggests that because tragedy possesses all the attributes of an epic, possibly possesses additional attributes such as spectacle and music, is more unified, and achieves the aim of its mimesis in shorter scope, it can be considered superior to epic.[78]

Aristotle was a keen systematic collector of riddles, folklore, and proverbs; he and his school had a special interest in the riddles of the Delphic Oracle and studied the fables of Aesop.[79]

Views on women

Aristotle's analysis of procreation describes an active, ensouling masculine element bringing life to an inert, passive female element. On this ground, feminist metaphysics have accused Aristotle of misogyny[80] and sexism.[81] However, Aristotle gave equal weight to women's happiness as he did to men's, and commented in his Rhetoric that the things that lead to happiness need to be in women as well as men.[82]

Loss and preservation of his works

Modern scholarship reveals that Aristotle's "lost" works stray considerably in characterization[83] from the surviving Aristotelian corpus. Whereas the lost works appear to have been originally written with an intent for subsequent publication, the surviving works do not appear to have been so.[83] Rather the surviving works mostly resemble lecture notes unintended for publication.[83] The authenticity of a portion of the surviving works as originally Aristotelian is also today held suspect, with some books duplicating or summarizing each other, the authorship of one book questioned and another book considered to be unlikely Aristotle's at all.[83]

Some of the individual works within the corpus, including the Constitution of Athens, are regarded by most scholars as products of Aristotle's "school," perhaps compiled under his direction or supervision. Others, such as On Colors, may have been produced by Aristotle's successors at the Lyceum, e.g., Theophrastus and Straton. Still others acquired Aristotle's name through similarities in doctrine or content, such as the De Plantis, possibly by Nicolaus of Damascus. Other works in the corpus include medieval palmistries and astrological and magical texts whose connections to Aristotle are purely fanciful and self-promotional.[84]

According to a distinction that originates with Aristotle himself, his writings are divisible into two groups: the "exoteric" and the "esoteric".[85] Most scholars have understood this as a distinction between works Aristotle intended for the public (exoteric), and the more technical works intended for use within the Lyceum course / school (esoteric).[86] Modern scholars commonly assume these latter to be Aristotle's own (unpolished) lecture notes (or in some cases possible notes by his students).[87] However, one classic scholar offers an alternative interpretation. The 5th century neoplatonist Ammonius Hermiae writes that Aristotle's writing style is deliberately obscurantist so that "good people may for that reason stretch their mind even more, whereas empty minds that are lost through carelessness will be put to flight by the obscurity when they encounter sentences like these."[88]

Another common assumption is that none of the exoteric works is extant – that all of Aristotle's extant writings are of the esoteric kind. Current knowledge of what exactly the exoteric writings were like is scant and dubious, though many of them may have been in dialogue form. (Fragments of some of Aristotle's dialogues have survived.) Perhaps it is to these that Cicero refers when he characterized Aristotle's writing style as "a river of gold";[89] it is hard for many modern readers to accept that one could seriously so admire the style of those works currently available to us.[87] However, some modern scholars have warned that we cannot know for certain that Cicero's praise was reserved specifically for the exoteric works; a few modern scholars have actually admired the concise writing style found in Aristotle's extant works.[90]

One major question in the history of Aristotle's works, then, is how were the exoteric writings all lost, and how did the ones we now possess come to us[91] The story of the original manuscripts of the esoteric treatises is described by Strabo in his Geography and Plutarch in his Parallel Lives.[92] The manuscripts were left from Aristotle to his successor Theophrastus, who in turn willed them to Neleus of Scepsis. Neleus supposedly took the writings from Athens to Scepsis, where his heirs let them languish in a cellar until the 1st century BC, when Apellicon of Teos discovered and purchased the manuscripts, bringing them back to Athens. According to the story, Apellicon tried to repair some of the damage that was done during the manuscripts' stay in the basement, introducing a number of errors into the text. When Lucius Cornelius Sulla occupied Athens in 86 BC, he carried off the library of Apellicon to Rome, where they were first published in 60 BC by the grammarian Tyrannion of Amisus and then by the philosopher Andronicus of Rhodes.[93][94]

Carnes Lord attributes the popular belief in this story to the fact that it provides "the most plausible explanation for the rapid eclipse of the Peripatetic school after the middle of the third century, and for the absence of widespread knowledge of the specialized treatises of Aristotle throughout the Hellenistic period, as well as for the sudden reappearance of a flourishing Aristotelianism during the first century B.C."[95] Lord voices a number of reservations concerning this story, however. First, the condition of the texts is far too good for them to have suffered considerable damage followed by

Apellicon's inexpert attempt at repair.

Second, there is "incontrovertible evidence," Lord says, that the treatises were in circulation during the time in which Strabo and Plutarch suggest they were confined within the cellar in Scepsis. Third, the definitive edition of Aristotle's texts seems to have been made in Athens some fifty years before Andronicus supposedly compiled his. And fourth, ancient library catalogues predating Andronicus' intervention list an Aristotelian corpus quite similar to the one we currently possess. Lord sees a number of post-Aristotelian interpolations in the Politics, for example, but is generally confident that the work has come down to us relatively intact.

On the one hand, the surviving texts of Aristotle do not derive from finished literary texts, but rather from working drafts used within Aristotle's school, as opposed, on the other hand, to the dialogues and other "exoteric" texts which Aristotle published more widely during his lifetime. The consensus is that Andronicus of Rhodes collected the esoteric works of Aristotle's school which existed in the form of smaller, separate works, distinguished them from those of Theophrastus and other Peripatetics, edited them, and finally compiled them into the more cohesive, larger works as they are known today.[96]

Legacy

More than 2300 years after his death, Aristotle remains one of the most influential people who ever lived. He contributed to almost every field of human knowledge then in existence, and he was the founder of many new fields. According to the philosopher Bryan Magee, "it is doubtful whether any human being has ever known as much as he did".[97] Among countless other achievements, Aristotle was the founder of formal logic,[98] pioneered the study of zoology, and left every future scientist and philosopher in his debt through his contributions to the scientific method.[99][100]

Despite these achievements, the influence of Aristotle's errors is considered by some to have held back science considerably. Bertrand Russell notes that "almost every serious intellectual advance has had to begin with an attack on some Aristotelian doctrine". Russell also refers to Aristotle's ethics as "repulsive", and calls his logic "as definitely antiquated as Ptolemaic astronomy". Russell notes that these errors make it difficult to do historical justice to Aristotle, until one remembers how large of an advance he made upon all of his predecessors.[4]

Later Greek philosophers

The immediate influence of Aristotle's work was felt as the Lyceum grew into the Peripatetic school. Aristotle's notable students included Aristoxenus, Dicaearchus, Demetrius of Phalerum, Eudemos of Rhodes, Harpalus, Hephaestion, Meno, Mnason of Phocis, Nicomachus, and Theophrastus. Aristotle's influence over Alexander the Great is seen in the latter's bringing with him on his expedition a host of zoologists, botanists, and researchers. He had also learned a great deal about Persian customs and traditions from his teacher. Although his respect for Aristotle was diminished as his travels made it clear that much of Aristotle's geography was clearly wrong, when the old philosopher released his works to the public, Alexander complained "Thou hast not done well to publish thy acroamatic doctrines; for in what shall I surpass other men if those doctrines wherein I have been trained are to be all men's common property?"[101]

Influence on Byzantine scholars

Greek Christian scribes played a crucial role in the preservation of Aristotle by copying all the extant Greek language manuscripts of the corpus. The first Greek Christians to comment extensively on Aristotle were John Philoponus, Elias, and David in the sixth century, and Stephen of Alexandria in the early seventh century.[102] John Philoponus stands out for having attempted a fundamental critique of Aristotle's views on the eternity of the world, movement, and other elements of Aristotelian thought.[103] After a hiatus of several centuries, formal commentary by Eustratius and Michael of Ephesus reappears in the late eleventh and early twelfth centuries, apparently sponsored by Anna Comnena.[104]

Influence on Islamic theologians

Aristotle was one of the most revered Western thinkers in early Islamic theology. Most of the still extant works of Aristotle,[105] as well as a number of the original Greek commentaries, were translated into Arabic and studied by Muslim philosophers, scientists and scholars. Averroes, Avicenna and Alpharabius, who wrote on Aristotle in great depth, also influenced Thomas Aquinas and other Western Christian scholastic philosophers. Alkindus considered Aristotle as the outstanding and unique representative of philosophy[106] and Averroes spoke of Aristotle as the "exemplar" for all future philosophers.[107] Medieval Muslim scholars regularly described Aristotle as the "First Teacher".[108] The title "teacher" was first given to Aristotle by Muslim scholars, and was later used by Western philosophers (as in the famous poem of Dante) who were influenced by the tradition of Islamic philosophy.[109]

In accordance with the Greek theorists, the Muslims considered Aristotle to be a dogmatic philosopher, the author of a closed system, and believed that Aristotle shared with Plato essential tenets of thought. Some went so far as to credit Aristotle himself with neo-Platonic metaphysical ideas.[105]

Influence on Western Christian theologians

With the loss of the study of ancient Greek in the early medieval Latin West, Aristotle was practically unknown there from c. AD 600 to c. 1100 except through the Latin translation of the Organon made by Boethius. In the twelfth and thirteenth centuries, interest in Aristotle revived and Latin Christians had translations made, both from Arabic translations, such as those by Gerard of Cremona,[110] and from the original Greek, such as those by James of Venice and William of Moerbeke.

After Thomas Aquinas wrote his theology, working from Moerbeke's translations, the demand for Aristotle's writings grew and the Greek manuscripts returned to the West, stimulating a revival of Aristotelianism in Europe that continued into the Renaissance.[111] Aristotle is referred to as "The Philosopher" by Scholastic thinkers such as Thomas Aquinas. See Summa Theologica, Part I, Question 3, etc. These thinkers blended Aristotelian philosophy with Christianity, bringing the thought of Ancient Greece into the Middle Ages. It required a repudiation of some Aristotelian principles for the sciences and the arts to free themselves for the discovery of modern scientific laws and empirical methods. The medieval English poet Chaucer describes his student as being happy by having at his beddes heedTwenty bookes, clad in blak or reed,Of aristotle and his philosophie,[112] The Italian poet Dante says of Aristotle in the first circles of hell,

I saw the Master there of those who know,Amid the philosophic family,By all admired, and by all reverenced;There Plato too I saw, and Socrates,Who stood beside him closer than the rest.[113]

Post-Enlightenment thinkers

The German philosopher Friedrich Nietzsche has been said to have taken nearly all of his political philosophy from Aristotle.[114] However debatable this is, Aristotle rigid separated action from production, and argued for the deserved subservience of some people ("natural slaves"), and the natural superiority (virtue, arete) of others. It is Martin Heidegger, not Nietzsche, who elaborated a new interpretation of Aristotle, intended to warrant his deconstruction of scholastic and philosophical tradition. Ayn Rand accredited Aristotle as "the greatest philosopher in history" and cited him as a major influence on her thinking. More recently, Alasdair MacIntyre has attempted to reform what he calls the Aristotelian tradition in a way that is anti-elitist and capable of disputing the claims of both liberals and Nietzscheans.[115]

Printed in the USA
CPSIA information can be obtained
at www.ICGtesting.com
LVHW020417291223
767710LV00004B/365